in it for

NOTHING

SCOTT
BEASLEY

in it for

NOTHING

Pleasant W rd
A Division of WINEPRESS PUBLISHING

Printed in the United States of America

Packaged by Pleasant Word, a division of WinePress Publishing, PO Box 428, Enumclaw, WA 98022. The views expressed or implied in this work do not necessarily reflect those of Pleasant Word, a division of WinePress Publishing. Ultimate design, content, and editorial accuracy of this work are the responsibilities of the author.

Unless otherwise noted, all Scriptures are taken from the King James Version of the Bible.

The Problem of Pain by C.S. Lewis Copyright © C.S. Lewis Pte. Ltd. 1940. Extract reprinted by permission.

ISBN 1.4141.0024.8
Library of Congress Catalog Card Number: 2003110076

TABLE OF CONTENTS

PREFACE

This book is for those who want to honor God consistently through the difficulties of life. It is for those who are hurting or broken. I want to help you make sense of it all and respond more appropriately than ever to past, present, and future trials, heartaches and aggravations. You might not find this book helpful unless you truly desire to honor God with your life.

With so many books on Christian bookstore shelves addressing the delicate subject of suffering and trials, one might ask why yet another volume is needed. I have asked the same of myself. I do not anticipate that I will answer all of your questions nor settle the perpetual theological questions that have spawned many heated discussions in the halls of higher learning. These pages will not delve deeply into the issue of whether God allows or authors evil. Many people more intelligent than myself have accurately explored such topics regarding God's sovereignty. This work determines to answer biblically the *purpose* behind the evils and trials that touch the lives of God's children. I will work from the conviction that God both authors and allows adversity to touch His children. As we shall determine, the purpose remains the same.

I do not attempt to cover every purpose or to exhaust every issue regarding our pain and suffering. But when the Scriptures clearly reveal the overriding purpose for our trials, hopefully, you will gain a greater understanding regarding the proverbial question countless saints have asked our Father, "Why?" Ultimately, I hope you will find greater grace to honor God in your trials and to comfort others with the comfort you have received in Christ Jesus. I believe God will help many people with this book—to endure their trials in a God-honoring fashion.

God led me to write these words. If you have a personal relationship with Jesus Christ, I hope this work will enrich your spiritual pilgrimage and strengthen your resolve to "be stead-fast, immovable, always abounding in the work of the Lord" (1 Corinthians 15:58). If you do not know the Lord personally, I pray the words of these pages might be used by the Holy Spirit to move you into this glorious journey!

I give God the glory and the credit for all that is correctly delineated in this book. It is because of Jesus Christ that my mind is enlightened, my experience steadfast, and my heart so full of joy. May He help all of us to not expect less for ourselves than was true for our blessed Lord Jesus.

—Scott Beasley
Canton, Georgia
July 22, 2003

ACKNOWLEDGEMENTS

I thank my wife, Lisa, for her encouragement throughout this project. She is the embodiment of steadfast devotion to our Lord Jesus and is in it for nothing. Lisa and I dedicate this book to our sons, Brett, Baxter, Jackson and Carson, with the hope they will follow Jesus as Lord all of their lives. We are especially thankful for our pastor and church, Dr. Johnny Hunt and First Baptist Church, Woodstock, Georgia. They helped us enormously as we attended the University of Adversity. We were greatly helped by our parents as well.

Chapter 1

THE UNIVERSITY OF ADVERSITY

"For we are His workmanship created in Christ Jesus . . ."
(Ephesians 1:9)

There was a man named Job who lived in Ur many centuries ago. He was a righteous man and very wealthy as well. Just as we love our children, Job loved his. He must have been a very busy man, having seven sons and three daughters. The devil hated Job. Moreover, the devil hated God. Unknown to Job, Satan approached God's throne with a wicked accusation concerning him. Satan accused Job of loving God for the wrong reason saying, "Does Job fear God for nothing?" (Job 1:9). With lightning quickness and guided missile precision, Satan brought Job's world crumbling down all round him. He would soon bury every one of his precious children. Everything around Job was shattered—except his faith. Satan did not believe Job was *in it for nothing* with God.

Life can be so difficult, even in the day we are living. My wife answered the phone one afternoon to hear the voice of her favorite cousin crying and sharing with Lisa how badly she was feeling physically. Lisa had been telling me for several days of her concern for her cousin Tammy. Ken and Tammy had been married for nearly 12 years when the Lord blessed them with the pregnancy of their third child. They were a godly young couple, serving the Lord faithfully. The third time was a "charm" until it was time for the baby to be born. Tammy had been suffering from severe headaches for several weeks leading up to her due date. When she collapsed in their home late one night, Ken got her to the hospital as quickly as possible. The doctors diagnosed her with bacterial meningitis. With her mother unconscious and unaware of her illness, the baby was delivered by caesarian section a short time later. Tammy did not live to see her baby. I shall never forget going to see her in the ICU. The doctors had just pronounced her dead. The sight of that tiny baby lying on the chest of her mother's lifeless body will be etched in my mind as long as I live. Ken and Tammy were faithful servants of the Lord Jesus Christ. It leaves one to wonder how God could allow such heartaches to touch the lives of His faithful children. Having been a pastor, I have seen my share of such tragedies.

The Christian life is an incredible, exciting journey with God Almighty. I enjoy life, and I love serving the Lord Jesus Christ. Several years ago, God gave me my life's objective, "To lift highly the gospel banner of Jesus Christ, raised with the pole of integrity and zeal, and flying stiffly in the wind of the Holy Spirit's power." More than anything else in life, this desire is my top priority. As I have walked with God for the past 17 years, I have seen Him do many wonderful things in my life and through my life. Life is wonderful because God is wonderful. However, as I ponder my Christian experience, I am sure the most difficult times in my life have induced the most fruitful times. It has not been easy to keep the gospel banner raised highly for those around me to see. I think of the apostle Peter when he stepped out of that boat to do something he had never done before. He experienced the gravity-defying power of God as he walked on water. He gazed at the Lord Jesus and walked on water, becoming a buoyant disciple unto the glory of God. Unfortunately, his gaze toward Jesus soon became a glance as he became distracted by the water beginning to rage around his calves. When he began to sink, Peter no longer honored the God he was so desirous to serve.

The devil is going to do all he can to stir the tempest in our lives. Have you ever wondered why God does not go ahead and cast Satan into his eternal abode? Erwin Lutzer writes, "If we ask why Satan has not already been consigned to the pit, the answer is that God is using him to complete the divine plan. He served before he fell and he is serving even now." [1] The devil belongs to God, and the Lord is using him to fulfill eternal purposes that often involve us. Satan will bring many types of storms into our lives. Some are relational, and others are financial. Some are spiritual, and others physical. Often, they are emotional and at times they concern our material possessions. The devil's activity in our lives can make it a real challenge to keep the gospel banner raised highly with boldness and consistency. The adversary attempts to deplete our resolve or diminish our confidence in the God we so love and desire to honor.

In this book, I will discuss some of the challenges we face in keeping the banner raised. We will delve into the Word of God in search of a biblical answer for the times we have asked God, "Why?" It is an awesome experience to walk with Jesus Christ through the twists and turns of this crazy phenomenon called life. Some Christians live in the survival mode, merely seeking to keep their heads above the water. Some live in what I term the contrival mode. They are always pulling themselves up by their own spiritual bootstraps and putting on the godly face at church. They have learned to appear patient and to come across as joyous. Though their lives are in shambles, they tell you they are fine. It is a contrived façade. Others live in what I call the thrival mode. They always seem to be doing well, spiritually thriving with God's bountiful supply of faith, fruit, and fortitude. It is not that their lives are free of trouble; rather, they have learned to depend on God's grace. Many of us meander in and out of the three modes. God has a better way. It is a victorious response that is founded upon the goodness and loving kindness of a personal God.

No matter which way the road might bend, the Christian life is not about contriving a façade of godliness. It is not about hanging on and merely surviving until the storm subsides. The Christian life God has in mind for us is about thriving by grace through faith. It is about trusting in Him. It is not about surviving but thriving on the sufficiency of God. You can thrive in the midst of a fiery furnace and bring immense honor to God in the process.

Has God ever allowed you to really hurt? If you live long enough as a follower of Jesus Christ, you will experience some difficult times. Someone asked, "What do you call a cow that has had its legs knocked out from under it?" The answer, "Ground beef." I realize that this joke is a bit juvenile, but may I ask you something personal? Have the circumstances of life ever knocked your feet out from under you? Have they ever knocked you to the ground? Most Christians are not desirous of encountering the adversities of life. I wonder about our approach to God at times. C. S. Lewis says, "We want, in fact, not so much a Father in Heaven as a grandfather in heaven—a senile benevolence who, as they say, 'liked to see young people enjoying themselves.'" [2] Most grandparents I know enjoy entertaining their grandchildren and spoiling them. We do not have a grandfather in heaven. We have our Father who sometimes allows the road of life to bend in hostile directions. If you have yet to encounter the cold winters of life, you will. These seasons afford us the opportunity to spit, quit, or develop Holy Ghost grit. We may spit in bitterness, quit in bewilderment, or exhibit true grit. As followers of Jesus Christ, we must bow before God with humble submission in order to portray the worthiness of our blessed Lord to be followed, regardless of what He may allow in our lives!

There is a school of higher, spiritual learning that all of us have attended at one time or another. It is a school like no other. Some of us have been full-time students, and some of us have attended part-time. I call this school the University of Adversity. The admission requirements to this university are unique— one must be born again. Speaking to His disciples, the Lord Jesus says, "In this world, you will have tribulation" (John 16:33). If you pass the admission requirement, there are two ways to become a student at the University of Adversity. Some students have enrolled themselves through ungodly living, for the Bible says, "Adversity pursues sinners" (Proverbs 13:21). On the other hand, some righteous saints have found themselves attending this school having been enrolled by Someone else. The Bible says, "For it is better, if God should will it so, that you suffer" (1 Peter 3:17). I want to address the latter group of people, for I have attended my share of classes at the University of Adversity.

As the sovereign God, He has the right to author and allow evil in this world. God has the right to allow it to be a world of woe. Have you ever understood the difference between evil and wicked? The Hebrew word for wickedness can be translated into calamity, sorrow, or wretchedness. Many times evil touches our lives as a result of sin. There are natural calamities that invade as well, and these ultimately result from sin—because we live in a fallen world. Evil is always purposed to fulfill, or bring about, the intentions and will of the Lord. Anytime an individual commits evil without this motive, we may call that evil wickedness. It is important for one to understand that God never commits wickedness, but He does send evil. Many would differ vehemently with me over this teaching, but I want to allow the Word of God to be the final word.

If you remove sinful connotations from your mind when you hear the word evil, you will understand the Bible when it speaks of God sending evil. The Bible has many references to God's connection with evil. Isaiah 45:7 says, "I form the light, and create darkness: I make peace, and create evil." Another poignant verse is found in Amos 3:6 where God explains, "Shall there be evil in a city and God hath not done it?" Other verses concur with these: Judges 2:15, Isaiah 31:2, Jeremiah 4:6, and Micah 1:12. At times, God is the author of evil. I want to make it very clear that His "evil" is not wicked, for it serves good and godly purposes. When mankind commits evil, it is known as wickedness. Man's evil is sinful and deserving of punishment for it does not have God's glory, honor, and purposes in view. The evil God initiates is different. He has an eternal, providential, sovereign plan in mind. His plan brings Him glory and honor. Though people might commit sin against us through unjust treatment and unmerited disfavor, God is using them to bring about His divine purposes. Those who bring evil are merely the rod and staff of God's choosing—to prune, primp, and promote us for His glory. He may want to prune ungodliness from our lives. It may be that He desires to portray the matchless power of His spiritual workmanship in saving and sanctifying us.

Yes, every follower of Jesus Christ will find himself attending the University of Adversity at one time or another. Some take easy courses; others may find themselves in way over their heads. Why do bad things happen to good people? How is it that you can be living according to God's will, serving Him wholeheartedly, and calamity comes in the midst of your faithfulness? If you feel bothered or upset after reading the opening pages of this book, please press through to the end. Regardless of the struggles we encounter in life, our God has much to do with them. You might argue the point, but God either authors or allows our troubles. Don't let this truth bother you. Our Lord Himself is the President of the University of Adversity, and is a graduate Himself—with honors! He was a "man of sorrows and acquainted with grief" (Isaiah 53:3). The Lord Jesus took the most challenging curriculum the university had to offer, even to death on a cross at Golgotha. He graduated at the very top of the class with an impeccable grade point average.

Dear child of God, so full of questions and disillusioned with life, the President of our university said, "A disciple is not above his teacher, nor a slave above his master" (Matthew 10:24). The Lord Jesus is telling us not to expect less of our experience in this life than was true of His. Jesus wants us to be willing to go where He went, to be what He was, and to endure what He encountered. Jesus wants us to be willing to be misunderstood or suffer when we have done everything right. This is a tough saying, and I am somewhat acquainted with the difficult and challenging ramifications of it.

One is more apt to learn what really matters when God batters, shatters, and splatters us. I can say that from personal experience. My journey as a follower of Jesus Christ actually began as a college student at the University of Georgia where I was an average student and an extraordinary sinner. My parents

17

took me to church during the first seven years of my life, but our attendance grew more and more sparse during my junior and high school years. When I was eleven, I tried to make grandma proud by "joining the church" and being baptized. I remember taking a change of clothes and showing up for the baptismal service only to leave that night as empty in my heart as ever. No one showed me how to receive Jesus Christ into my heart. I can count on both hands the number of times I darkened the doors of a church from that night until the day God saved me. And, believe me, I darkened the doors!

My heart grew emptier over the years, especially as I entered college. One way I tried to fill the emptiness of my heart was by joining a reputable fraternity on campus. I shall not forget the night three men from a campus ministry (Campus Crusade for Christ) visited our fraternity house during dinner and shared the gospel with over 100 lost young men. The Holy Spirit began to convict my heart as they shared the story of Jesus Christ's death on the cross and His victorious resurrection. I was one of four or so men who accepted their invitation to again for more information. We met a few days later on campus at the Tate Student Center. I clung to my meaningless baptismal experience, as again they shared the gospel of Jesus' death and resurrection. Their ministry moved me closer, but I rejected their invitation to receive Jesus. I remember walking across campus that day knowing in my heart that I was lost and without God. I knew I did not have what (who) they were talking about, but I was not ready.

Soon after those close encounters of a spiritual kind, I made my way home to Atlanta for Easter break. My daddy asked me to go with him to pick up my mother's car from the shop. We stopped for an ice cream on the way, and it was there that my dad began telling me of his newfound understanding and faith in Jesus Christ. I was shocked and a caught totally off guard by his witness. I listened carefully as he shared his salvation experience, all the while counting the cost in my mind. I knew a decision to follow the Lord would mean some radical changes for my life and have huge ramifications for my social life. I had been helping to manage a liquor store for nearly two years and had just started an enjoyable stint as a varsity cheerleader with the Bulldogs. I knew the relationship with the young lady I was dating would never last unless she received the Lord as well. But the Holy Spirit continued to move lovingly and patiently in my life until I was brought to the end of myself in October 1985. Never will I forget kneeling beside my bed in that Athens' apartment and giving my heart to the Lord Jesus Christ. The change in my life was instantaneous and radical. For the first time, I had real peace in my heart. I experienced the true meaning in life and profound contentment. The Holy Spirit wrought some major moral changes in my heart as well.

I soon realized God's plan for my life was in full-time vocational ministry. I met my wife Lisa shortly before graduating from the University of Georgia in 1987. We were married the following year and moved to Memphis, Tennessee, to attend seminary. We had the privilege of serving on staff at a church in Memphis for over three years, until we both graduated from the seminary. Shortly after graduation in 1992, we began a new ministry with another church in Mississippi. By this time, Lisa was pregnant with our first child. I will never forget the day I stopped by our home for a moment to check on something, only to discover Lisa standing in the kitchen looking very distraught. When I asked her what was wrong, she replied, "I think I have lost my water." My first thought was, "Darling, you're in the kitchen, just pour you another glass." Being in her twenty-fourth week of pregnancy, we were very concerned at the possibility that she had lost her amniotic fluid.

We called her doctor who was nearly two hours away, and he told us to get to his office quickly. After diagnosing our situation, he reported that indeed Lisa had lost eighty percent of her water, and that both she and the baby were in a dangerous situation. The doctor gave us three choices: 1) travel to Missouri and have an abortion, 2) let nature take its course, 3) get a prescription for Brethene that would help stop the contractions or buy time. Of course, we accepted the latter proposition, and Lisa began total bed rest at the home of some dear friends in Memphis.

We were in their home nearly six days when I heard Lisa screaming from the bedroom. As I entered the room, she informed me that the baby was beginning to appear. That's when I loaded her in the car and began the longest twenty-minute car ride I had ever experienced. Twenty-five minutes after arriving at Baptist East Hospital, Lisa gave birth to a one pound, eleven ounce boy. Brett was given a ten percent chance of making it through the night. God allowed him to live. After four days of losing weight, he weighed nearly thirteen ounces! For the next two and a half months, we drove 100 miles one-way to see our baby struggle for his life. We wanted to be there every day, but the distance prohibited us. Our hearts and minds were there.

This was not the way life was supposed to work out for someone who had allowed God to save them, agreed to become His representative in Christian ministry, uprooted and attended seminary, and had been used of God to make a wonderful impact for the Lord. Brett was in the hospital nearly two and one half months when the doctors released him, weighing just over four pounds. We have always believed the physicians allowed him to go home too soon. But we did not share our concerns vehemently. For the next ten months, Brett wore a heart monitor because premature babies have a high propensity for sleep apnea. I cannot count the times we heard that little box sounding its alarm in the middle of the night. Many times we rushed in to discover him lying there with blue shaded lips and not breathing. These sleep-deprived months seemed to last an eternity.

Meanwhile, our pastor and church were extremely support-ive and helpful. They had waited two years to fill the position we had accepted. Our ministry there was in its fifth week when all of this began. My heart was torn. They needed and deserved a dynamic youth ministry, and my heart was not in it for more than one reason. A couple of years earlier, I had shared my grow-ing desire with my pastor in Memphis to start and pastor a church. About six months after Brett came home, I shared this same vision with my pastor in Mississippi. The next year, Lisa and I left that comfortable position to move to Atlanta, Geor-gia, to start a new ministry. We did not have money, a savings account, or health insurance, but we did have the call of God. We rented a house and began a Bible study on Wednesday nights. The ministry started with seven people, including Brett in the nursery. By the end of that year, we moved the ministry to a government-owned building just down the road. The ministry seemed to be growing in every way. God's Spirit was saving people and adding people to the church nearly every week.

When Lisa became pregnant the next year with our second child, the church was averaging seventy-five people in her wor-ship services. The year was 1995, and Lisa was in her twenty-fifth week of pregnancy. I will never forget having dinner with some friends when the pager sounded showing my home phone number. I phoned Lisa, and she told me that I needed to get home quickly. Something reminiscent of her pregnancy with Brett was beginning to occur. By the time I arrived, it was ap-parent that we must get to a doctor, preferably her doctor. Be-cause of our prior experience with a premature birth, Lisa had been seeing a doctor specializing in high-risk pregnancies. We lived forty-five minutes from the hospital, and my nerves were on edge as we traveled hastily into downtown Atlanta. Lisa's contractions were coming every two minutes, and we were only half way there. Upon arriving that evening, the doctors in the emergency room admitted Lisa at ten-thirty. The night was long as the physicians tried to stop what seemed to be inevitable.

The next morning, Lisa birthed our second child weighing two pounds, six ounces. Leah was a precious baby girl. Her only problem was that she looked like her daddy. Unlike the first premature delivery, Lisa was uneasy about this episode. She had tested positive as a carrier of beta-streptococcus, a bacteria that can spawn a myriad of problems. The doctors were not able to administer the antibiotics needed in order to preclude problems before Lisa delivered Leah. The baby had gotten into the birth canal before she received the medication. Leah's development progressed without a hitch for nearly a month and a half. It was interesting to watch the nurses remove that small baby from her incubator and bathe her tiny body. She was not too small or weak to express her displeasure.

Leah weighed nearly five pounds the day I received a frantic phone call from my mother telling me to get to the hospital as soon as possible. I arrived to be greeted by Lisa with tears flowing down her cheeks. Leah had contracted bacterial meningitis, a brutal disease that attacks the lining of the brain. Leah remained in a comatose state for nearly a week with only a possible hint of any brain activity. The attending physician in the neo-natal unit told us it was time to make a decision to disconnect Leah from life support. We followed him to his office. If we had not been numbed already by the emotions of the moment, we would have been by the cold air-conditioning pouring into his windowless office. As we sat down, I remember his

Romanian accented voice saying, "This is a form commanding us not to resuscitate, to aid Leah's life, or to prolong it. If she has a problem, we will do nothing." Reaching for his pen to sign the form, I felt as though I was killing my little girl. How could I feel like this was best for her? I reluctantly signed it. Lisa signed the command after me.

I felt like I had just killed my daughter. We visited again the next day before the order was to be implemented the following day. As Lisa held Leah, she began to tenderly kiss her forehead. Each time, Leah seemed to open one of her eyes halfway and close it again. We became so excited and called the nurses over. They told us it was a reflex. We always believed God gave us that tender, precious experience on that hot, Thursday afternoon in June.

Suddenly, our hopes were quickly dashed as Lisa held Leah tenderly in her arms. Leah's complexion began changing colors as if she were a chameleon. Lisa frantically cried out, "What's wrong with her? What's wrong with her?" The nurses rushed to us and, one began to put oxygen to the baby's face. I saw a large hand penetrating that group of nurses as the doctor pushed the oxygen back and said, "No more." Leah died moments later, held in the loving arms of her mother and under the watchful eyes of her daddy. Her funeral was conducted the following Sunday, which happened to be Father's Day. When other pastors were leaving their churches to have lunch with their children, we were going to bury a baby daughter. I will always be grateful for two dear pastors and friends, Dr. Johnny Hunt and Dr. Chuck Herring, for giving their time on Father's Day to lead the funeral service. Phil Weatherwax, our former pastor from First Baptist Church, Grenada, Mississippi, was there as well. Our church family, West Cobb Baptist Church, was very supportive. Nevertheless, Lisa and I were going through a heart-wrenching time. It was very sad.

Lisa and I were students in the University of Adversity! We met at a secular university, and now we were at another university—a spiritual one. Perhaps you can imagine that there were many times I wanted to transfer to another school. The University of Adversity is not as fun or appealing as the University of Pleasurability. At the time, the University of Ease, Comfort, and Pleasure sounded good. Although I have yet to graduate, I can tell you that there is much profit from attending the University of Adversity. *It is a privilege God entrusts to us.*

Jesus' twelve disciples attended the same school. One class they took was Storms 101. The story is recorded in the Gospel of Mark 4:35–41. While the Lord Jesus was asleep in their boat, the disciples found themselves in the throes of a turbulent storm on the sea. After He was awakened by the frightened men and had calmed the storm, the Bible says something very important. In Mark 4:40–41, Jesus says, "'Why are you so timid? How is it that you have no faith?' And they became very afraid and said to one another, 'Who then is this, that even the wind and the sea obey Him?'"

Gaze with me through the window of God's Word into their classroom. Notice all of the learning occurring in Storms 101 that day! Others, without Jesus in their boats, learned about them. Verse 36 says, "Other boats were with Him." From their boats, those other students watched the disciples as they responded to the storm. They learned that the disciples of the Miracle Worker were not at all like the One they followed. I wonder how often we forget that other people are watching our lives. Let me hasten to say that this fact should not be the first and primary factor driving our response to adversity. God sees, and this alone is enough for us to be careful. But people are watching our lives. They want to see how real we are.

Gaze into that window again and notice that the disciples learned something about themselves. Jesus revealed and pronounced their spiritual ineptness when He called them timid and critiqued the depth of their faith. Even if others do not learn something about us through the difficulties of life, we ought to pay careful attention. The Lord revealed to them what He already knew of them—they had room to grow in faith. I believe their storm became a classroom where the Master Teacher taught them what we cannot know lest God reveals it . . . our hearts. Jeremiah 17:9 teaches our inability to know our hearts, except God reveals what He knows to be true.

Mark 4 reveals three types of learning through the storm. The disciples learned about themselves. Others learned about the disciples. Some learned about Jesus. Their newfound revelation of the Lord Jesus caused them to question the kind of man He was! They learned about God. The most important thing to look for during your trials is a newfound understanding and knowledge of who He is.

From within the storms and difficulties I have encountered, God has begun to teach me something of paramount importance as a child of God. God wants me to weather the storms He allows in my life by looking to Him to do at least one of three things during the storm. I am always looking for Him to prove my faith, improve my future, or remove my fortress. Storms are an opportunity for God to reveal the genuineness of my faith. They reveal whether I am real. Storms are an opportunity for God to better my future. Joseph went to Egypt in slavery and became the leader of the country, only second to Pharoah (Genesis 41:40). Storms give me the opportunity to witness the power of God as He sometimes removes the fortresses Satan erects before me. These fortresses are circumstances too great for me to handle. They are situations that extend beyond the ability of my flesh to rescue, remove, or rewrite. They drive me to God and provide opportunities for Him to once again demonstrate His divine, dynamic power! I have seen Him remove many fortresses!

On a personal level, may I ask how will you ever be a bright and bold witness for the Lord Jesus Christ if you have not personally learned He is who He says He is in the Word of God? How will you personally know He is Jehovah Rapha, the Lord our Healer, if you have never needed healing? How could you ever proclaim to the world with intensity and integrity that He is Jehovah Shalom, The Lord our Peace, if you never encounter a time of insecurity and uncertainty? It might be that many of the Lord's disciples are not on fire for the Lord because they have not seen Him save them from the fire of life's troubles. The more we see Him doing in our lives, the more apt we are to be talking to others about Him!

What is your problem today? Is there an obstacle standing in your way? Every obstacle we encounter can be handled through God or dismantled by God. Therefore, every obstacle is an opportunity. They are opportunities for God to show how great, awesome, and almighty He is! Thank God for the opportunities!

Remember the disciples in the boat? The University of Adversity can be a difficult school to attend, but there is much to be learned if you will stay in the boat with Jesus. Others saw them; they saw themselves; they saw God! Everyone learned something through that storm! C. S. Lewis was correct in saying, "God shouts through our pain."[3] He also whispers. He speaks. Storms are a theatre of learning, and the teacher is the

Holy Spirit of God. All too often, God has shown me I am not a good student. Have you ever attended the University of Adversity? Are you currently taking classes there? What does the university President think of your grades? What kind of student are you? The rest of this book is written to help you become a valedictorian.

Chapter 2

PERCEPTION DECEPTION

Your attitude toward adversity will make or break you. You probably have some things in your life that you consider as negative, while God views them as good. Some people view trials as the black velvet on which they are privileged to display the diamond of God's grace and goodness. Others view adversity antithetically as an inconvenience to and interruption of the plan they have for their lives. All too often, the problem is with perception. Sometimes the *is* seems to be *isn't*. At other times, the *isn't* seems to be *is*. The devil loves to deceive us into believing reality isn't reality. Our struggles with depression, disappointment, and other like symptoms are often connected with our perception of life. Satan wins the battle for proper perspective by leading us to think reality is not reality and unreality is reality. I do not understand everything about the devil, but the Bible teaches he has been given the ability to masquerade and deceive (2 Corinthians 11:14). Max Anders states, "He can make poison taste like candy."[1] I call this perception deception.

When Lisa and I graduated from seminary, we interviewed with a pastor search committee in Georgia. I preached for them on a Sunday morning at a church, and we met them for lunch afterwards. Although we spent the whole afternoon with them, one person on the committee would hardly look at me all day. I quit trying to establish any conversation with this individual after several attempts. Later in the day, I remarked to Lisa how much that one person on the committee seemed to dislike me. For other reasons, we did not accept the invitation to pastor their church. Several weeks passed, and I received a letter from the same person on the committee. Tears formed in my eyes as I read those six pages of adulation, admiration, and encouragement. After reading the letter, one would have thought I was the next Billy Graham. That was over ten years ago, and I still have the note. I have saved it for encouragement. I was so wrong. You have to be careful about the way you perceive things. Often, you are wrong.

In the 1990's, there was a commercial advertisement with the catch phrase, "Attitude is everything." Well, attitude is *not* everything, but it is crucial. What determines our attitudes is of utmost importance. Attitude is determined by how we perceive things, and our perception must be based upon the Word of God. The apostle Paul wrote in 2 Corinthians 12:10, "Therefore I take pleasure in infirmities, in reproaches, in necessities, in persecution, in distresses for Christ's sake: for when I am weak, then I am strong." Note Paul's attitude toward adversity, "I take pleasure." He had an uncommon and unnatural attitude. His winning attitude was based upon a perception that God would provide what was needed. His perception was founded upon the Word of God. The Holy Spirit inspired Paul to write, "For when I am weak, then I am strong." In other words, Paul believed if God led him in, then God would lead him out. If God led him to it, then God would lead him through it!

Circumstances in life can leave us feeling weak, can't they? They can be so difficult. The psalmist Asaph wrote a song about his disturbed, wrestling spirit. Psalm 73 reveals a man with perception deception. He was distraught over the seeming prosperity of the wicked versus that of the godly. He perception deception is recognizable because of his spiritual delusion. Verses 1–5 reveal his deluded convictions regarding the prosperity of the wicked.

Psalm 73:1–5 states, "Truly God is good to Israel, even to such as are of a clean heart. But as for me, my feet were almost gone; my steps had well nigh slipped. For I was envious at the foolish, when I saw the wicked. For there are no bands in their death: but their strength is firm. They are not in trouble as other men; neither are they plagued like other men."

Asaph's theology about the holiness of God and goodness of God was under attack. He perceived the situation in an unbiblical manner. He had perception deception. Never forget what God says to you in Philippians 4:7 about the result of prayerfulness. "And the peace of God, which surpasses all comprehension, shall guard your hearts and *minds* in Christ Jesus." If the devil can get your thinking out of bounds with the Word of God, he has won a great victory against your pursuit of godliness. Asaph was deluded into thinking those without God were doing better than those with God.

Read Psalm 73 again, paying close attention to verses 10–14. Asaph was confused—something God never authors in His children. God's Word says,

Therefore his people return hither: and waters of a full cup are wrung out to them. And they say, 'How doth God know? And is there knowledge in the most High? Behold these are the ungodly, who prosper in the world; they increased in riches. Verily I have cleansed my heart in vain, and washed my hands in innocency. For all day long have I been plagued, and chastened every morning.

Asaph just did not get it. How could the unrighteous slap a holy God in the face and prosper while God chastened him as he sought to honor God? No wonder he was so full of confusion. He was full of delusion about God's fairness and goodness to His children. Asaph's perception of circumstances around him was wrong. He viewed them through the lenses of deception fed by the lies of the devil. God's Word says, "Do not be deceived, God is not mocked. What a man sows, that he will also reap" (Galatians 6:7). Asaph needed to give God time to allow the seeds of their sin to germinate and produce the fruit of unwanted consequences. Given enough time, they would be drowning in the waters of their folly.

But Asaph came to his senses, and God brought him through his bout with perception deception. Psalm 73:16–17 states, "When I thought to know this, it was too painful for me; until I went into the sanctuary of God; then understood their end." Intimate fellowship with Jesus is the cure for perception deception. If you fail to remain connected with Christ in intimate fellowship, you will be very susceptible to the deceptive work of Satan.

Can you hear the tidal wave of emotions rushing through the heart and mind of a mother and father receiving the shocking news that their daughter and son were killed in an accident involving their church van as they were en route to summer camp? Do you hear the thoughts and fears of a wife as she reads an anonymous note from someone saying, "Call this number, and I'll tell you whom your husband has been sleeping with." Are you able to fathom the deep sense of loss rushing through a man as he turns in bed early in the morning to discover his childhood sweetheart has died in the night, having shared 55 years of life as husband and wife? Real moments like these come into our lives, often catching us totally by surprise. Our perception of our circumstances can become very confused and distorted. How we perceive them determines how we respond to them. The lens through which you view your life will determine the response you make in light of it.

Satan often employs a scheme to thwart God's plan for our lives that would consequently honor the Lord. The devil likes to implement perception deception. If the devil can distort your perception of God, then he has won the battle. If he can distort our view of what God is doing and allowing around us, he has gone a long way in disrupting the vitality in our walk with God. There is a dear, beloved evangelist named Junior Hill who once preached a message about perception. In the middle of his sermon, his cell phone began to ring. He asked us to excuse him for a moment, wondering if the call was from his wife. He answered the phone and began conversing, apparently with his wife. He told her he was in the middle of preaching at the conference and asked if all was well. He eventually got back to his sermon. Sometime later, as he was talking about perception, he let us in on the fact that the cell phone in his coat was actually a toy. He drove home the point. What you think you see is not always what you see. The way you think things are is not always the way things are. Sometimes what you think is, isn't. Sometimes what you think isn't, is.

Study the circumstances and, more importantly, the attitude of a biblical character named Joseph who found himself in the throes of injustice and adversity. Joseph was sold into slavery by his brothers. He was taken to foreign land where, in Egypt, he soon found himself in prison for no apparent reason. He was falsely accused of raping a woman. However, the Bible reveals Joseph's response as upright, faithful, and positive. Despite the problems he encountered, Joseph maintained a repetitive sequence of promotions and kept rising out of his adversity with astounding honor. Every problem became a chance for promotion. His brothers sold him into slavery, and he was taken to Egypt. Although he was taken down to Egypt, God raised him up in Egypt! He was later consigned to prison, but God assigned him as leader of the nation, second only to Pharoah in power. He responded well in attitude and actions because he had the correct perception toward life. After his ascension to power in Egypt, Joseph encountered his brothers. Joseph's perception is revealed as he attempts to preclude their apologies saying, "You meant it for evil, but God meant it for good."

I want you to think about something with me. Do you think Joseph developed this perspective after his promotions or before? Did his perception toward his plight in life become reminiscent of Romans 8:28, only after the Lord raised him above and beyond the injustice? I am sure Joseph's preconceived perception toward life was only later revealed in his words to his brothers. There was no indication that Joseph had to learn this difficult, yet glorious, lesson. God had placed His Word in principle within Joseph, and this guided his heart from battle to battle, from victory to victory. Joseph was spiritually malleable in that he trusted God to guard, guide, and govern his life. God led him to it, and God led him through it! He will do the same for you. The Bible says, "Humble yourselves therefore under the mighty hand of God, that He may exalt you in due time: casting all your care upon Him; for He careth for you" (1 Peter 5:6–7).

When God saved me, my heart resonated with the truth that Jesus is God and, if He is living in my heart, then I can trust Him to guard my life. God is sovereign and almighty; therefore, I know He will guide the affairs of my life. He has a plan for my life. Jesus can and will govern my life because He is in control. He is the Good Shepherd. A shepherd worth his salt will put and keep the sheep where they need to be. A good shepherd is a faithful one, and he will guard and guide them. He will govern their entire existence. As the sheep of His pasture, we can be certain Jesus will govern, guard, and guide our lives. He will take care of us spiritually, emotionally, materially, socially, domestically, financially, economically, and physically. He is the Good Shepherd.

I have the deeply rooted conviction that if God loves me and is my personal Shepherd, then I can trust Him to take care of me, even when my circumstances seem to contradict that belief. I am not advocating a whatever-will-be, will-be philosophy for living the Christian life. Surely, we have not because we ask not. When you have done all that you can do, there is nothing left to do but trust God. My part is to live a holy, prayerful, Spirit-filled life, and trust God with what befalls me. The Bible says, "He withholds no good thing from those who walk uprightly" (Psalm 84:11). Even when God allows my life to go from bad to worse, from within the storm there remains the same promise. My perception does not fluctuate, based on circumstances. From within the storm, God withholds no good thing from me. If He keeps the storm at sea, He has been working for my good. If God allows the storm to make a direct hit on my life, God will see me through it. Every Christian should have an optimistic perspective. "God is faithful" (1 Corinthians

1:9). If you perceive your life in light of these truths, your perception toward the reception of adversity will be a positive influence that will compel you forward with strength and courage. You will advance through adversity unto the glory of God.

As God's child, I am a sheep of His fold. He is the Good Shepherd. The Lord Jesus Christ is capable of leading me into the good, green pastures of His perfect will. Not only is He capable, He is always leading me. According to Psalm 23, God is leading me into the places sheep like to go and, indeed, need to go. He is the Good Shepherd. This is the perception through which we are to view our lives. The devil will not tell you these truths. He will lie to you, twist the truth, and inject doubt into your heart and mind. If you tend to be easily discouraged, it is because you are not consistent in trusting God. Doubt is a sin when it progresses into unbelief. The line is crossed from doubt to unbelief when mere questions arising from shock or surprise progress into a lack of faith. The Bible says, "Without faith it is impossible to please God" (Hebrews 11:6). If you are not living by faith, then you are not pleasing God. You were created for His pleasure (Revelation 4); therefore, unbelief is a sin. I want to challenge you to trust God.

Perception deception is avoided most aptly when we embrace God's Word by faith and treasure it in our hearts. The truth of His Word determines perception. Perception determines perspective, and perspective determines attitude. Attitude determines response, and response determines the outcome, because your response will determine how you react to your circumstances. Reflect on your life and the way you respond to the small and large issues. How do you react? Are you guilty of living in perception deception?

Chapter 3

TROPHIES OF GRACE

The grades you receive at the University of Adversity are a reflection of your perception, attitude, and understanding toward the difficulties of life that God allows. I must ask you, "Have you once and for all embraced your past, present, and future troubles as a friend and ally of that which would bring God glory?" If not, whose glory are you seeking in life—yours or His?

Understand the heart God is putting in me. I want to be a faithful rebel with a cause. I want God to give me a heart that will accompany Him regardless of the circumstances of life. I desire, more than life itself, to be radically, fanatically, and overwhelmingly on fire for Jesus Christ. I want to be known as a disciple of Jesus Christ. I want people to know my true spiritual colors: quickly, definitively, and assuredly. I want the world to see the resulting power of the blood by which I am purchased. I hope this world sees the Lord Jesus Christ alive in me, His Holy Spirit lighting the brow of my heart with my life laid on the anvil of obedient sacrifice. I long to hear God call for the Isaacs of my life. With the faith of Abraham, I desire to see my heart willingly plunge the knife of sacrifice into anything I deem precious. I want to see the Lord keep my hand from those things, and only those things, that He would have me retain as alive unto me. I want to live as a man bought, for that is what I am. I do not want the circumstances of life to sap my spiritual fervor and anointing.

I thank the Lord Jesus for eternal life and for changing my heart and life. I want the reality of it and knowing Him to personally illumine me, consume me, and compel me into the life. I want the Lord to fuel the engines of my service with Holy Spirit power that can move the heaviest loads of sin and the most grievous mountains of heartache, and the most hopeless flatbeds of despair. I want God to use me to make His mark in the lives of people—people lost, people hurting, people searching, people mourning, and people in despair. I want to see the Lord Jesus use my life for the exact purpose for which He fashioned, saved and sent me.

I desire for the Lord Jesus to be above and beyond all my ambitions, aspirations, and attitudes—privately and publicly. He is my reason to live. I want Him, as my life and joy, to become evident to all. I want to be His man, living His plan, doing all I can through His Spirit's power. I want God to live through me, love through me, listen through me, and labor through me. I do not want merely the expected in my life, but the unexpected as well. I do not want merely the possible, but the impossible, accomplished through my life. I do not want merely the probable, but the improbable. I do not want merely the expected accomplished, but the unexpected. I want to dream His dreams, build His dreams, live His dreams and die pursuing His dreams.

I long to see God take His Word and dredge the muddy depths of my heart's sin and wickedness to clean the core of my existence, expand the potential of my present, and chart His course for my life. I want to live above the trials of this life in order to see God set my heart aflame with the distinguishable and inextinguishable passion for holiness and purely motivated zeal. I desire for those closest to me to see my fellowship with Him as evident and real. I long for the world to be impacted by this fire, eternally and in reality. I want the high density laser beam of His eternal Word to fuel my spirit into a lifestyle of prayerful intercession resulting in obedience, confession, adoration, holiness, evangelism, communion, love and, fruit that remains. This is what God is putting in my heart. This is my desire. It is His desire. I am saddened to admit that it is not my consistent testimony, nor is it the fragrance I gain from spending time in the garden of God's people—known as the church.

Few words describe many Christians today better than the word atrophy. Many believers and churches are atrophic in their personal growth in holiness and strength. K. P. Yohannan states that, "The spiritual temperature in many of our churches is so low right now that a new believer has to become a backslider to feel at home."[1] How many times have you seen an individual or a church go through difficult circumstances only to come through those challenges with less spiritual growth, fervor, and strength? The musical group *Newsboys* recorded a song entitled "Lost the Plot." The song describes Christians who have become relaxed in their spiritual devotion because God didn't fit their image, and they lost (forgot) the plot to Christian life. Just in case you have forgotten, the plot is to honor and glorify God! The song goes on to give the reason why many Christians lose the plot—God wouldn't play Santa Claus. How many followers of Jesus Christ are standing on the sidelines of the Christian life, allowing the devil squeeze his water bottle of bitterness deep into their souls, because God did not answer their prayers in the way they prayed He would?

The Ronco Company once produced some entertaining television commercials. Do you remember the elderly woman using her emergency alert gadget when she fell exiting her bathtub? She alerted the EMT by speaking into a transmitter and saying, "Help, I've fallen, and I can't get up." Another commercial featured the same woman lying in bed reading a book. When she decides to go to sleep, she doesn't even get out of bed or roll over to turn off the lights. Instead, she abruptly closes the book and claps her hands to turn off the bedroom lights. She had a clap-on, clap-off gadget. I doubt Ronco put a lot of financial backing into those commercials.

I have been in the ministry long enough to have witnessed a lot of Ronco Christians. Generally, they only seem to call on God when they have fallen and can't get up. They try to use God to make their lives more convenient. Ronco Christians think they can clap God on when they need Him and clap God off when they are finished with Him. When will they realize they need the Light of the world all the time? I have heard Pastor Johnny Hunt say, "God might use you, but you will never use God!"

Such attitudes toward God should be foreign to the children of God. We are trophies of His grace! Is it right that the One who made us trophies of His grace should receive such a response? The Bible says, "For we must all appear before the judgment seat of Christ, that each one may be recompensed for his deeds in the body, according to what he has done, whether good or bad" (2 Corinthians 5:10). Do you think that you will get a trophy for atrophy? Webster defines atrophy as a wasting away of body or parts. An individual with atrophy is underdeveloped and unhealthy. God wants to use adversity and the challenges of life to exercise our faith. He desires to produce spiritually fit followers.

Have you noticed how often the difficulties of life seem to have the common effect of turning believers away from the Lord (and thus against Him). I believe most Christians who allow their spiritual fervor to cool because of adversity do not understand the opportunity they have to demonstrate the sufficiency of God's grace, goodness and worthiness. They do not understand their responsibility as followers of the King of kings. If you have a personal relationship with God through Jesus Christ, 1 Peter 2:9 teaches that God saved you that you "may proclaim the excellencies of Him who has called you out of darkness into His marvelous light." We are saved to proclaim Him to the world. It is our responsibility and privilege now and for all eternity! It is the privilege and responsibility of every trophy of God's grace!

I am reminded of one such trophy that happened to be my grandmother. Before she went to be with the Lord, she told me how everything seemed normal on that Wednesday morning in May 1969, when she called my grandfather to breakfast. He did not respond as usual, so Grandmother walked into the doorway of his bedroom and called him again. Shaking his foot, Grandmother noticed the coolness of Granddaddy's body. She soon learned that God had ushered him into His presence during the night through a heart attack. Later, Grandmother found his Bible open to John's gospel with Granddad's Sunday school lesson for the next Sunday marking the spot. She found it lying open on the chest of drawers where Granddad had left it after studying the night before. Grandmother lamented as she remembered him just three months before saying, "I've cut my life short fifteen years by drinking beer and not going to church." Things had not always been so sweet and peaceful for them.

My daddy was about ten years old when he saw my granddad grabbing my grandmother in the kitchen by the hair of her head. She married my grandfather years before receiving Jesus as her Lord and Savior. God's grace quickly molded her heart into a devout and godly influence that was very contagious. But granddad's story is different. He was an evil-tempered man with an addiction to alcohol. Once, he chased my dad angrily through their home because he had fallen out of a tree and broken his collarbone. It was the only time my dad remembers my grandmother raising her voice to him, although she had untold opportunities to do so. But she endured, and she prayed. Grandmother shared, and she sought to be controlled by God's Spirit. She deeply desired for her godless husband to see the reality of the Lord and receive Him. My grandmother held on for thirty-five years through mental, emotional, and physical abuse.

While I do not recommend this tenacious devotion for every circumstance, my grandmother became evidence for Granddad as he ascertained the reality of Jesus Christ in her life. Realizing God's grace had won her to faith in 1935, Grandmother sought to live as a trophy displaying God's amazing grace. She was a trophy drawing attention to the wonderful God who had claimed her as His own! Granddad watched that trophy over the years and placed his faith in Jesus Christ just three months before he died. She became his excuse to get saved rather than his excuse to not get saved. I am certain that my granddad is in heaven today because of a woman who decided to live as to display the worthiness of the Lord, regardless of circumstances. Although God answered her prayers for my granddad's salvation long after she began praying, she chose to live as a trophy of God's grace. The life she lived gave credence to the sufficiency, goodness, and worthiness of God. As a moth is drawn in the darkness to the light, so was the soul of her husband drawn to Jesus Christ as she shined in such darkness over the years.

Every child of God must come to grips with whether they are going to preach through their trials. The sermon is the worthiness of God to be loved, followed, and obeyed, regardless of the circumstances He allows. Such thinking needs to originate and rest in a heart saturated and captivated by the Word of God. I want you to begin viewing yourself as a trophy of God's grace. What is a trophy? A trophy is something that serves as evidence of an accomplishment and a lasting reminder of it. That's what we are as God's children—trophies of His grace. If you have been saved, you are an eternal reminder to all creation that the Holy Spirit won the victory over your flesh, sin, and Satan. I am a lasting reminder of that grace, and God wants to display me on the mantle of eternity as evidence of His saving ability.

Why and how am I to see myself as a trophy? Consider the Bible in Ephesians 2:1–10.

> And you hath He quickened who were dead in trespasses and sins: wherein in time past you walked according to the course of this world, according to the prince of the power of the air, the spirit that now worketh in the children of disobedience: among whom also we all had our conversation in times past in the lusts of our flesh, fulfilling the desires of the flesh and of the mind; and were by nature the children of wrath, even as others. But God, who is rich in mercy, for His great love wherewith He loved us, even when we were dead in sins, hath quickened us together with Christ, (by grace you are saved;) and hath raised us up together, and made us sit together in heavenly places in Christ Jesus: that in the ages to come He might show the exceeding riches of His grace in His kindness toward us through Christ Jesus. For by grace are you saved through faith; and that not of yourselves: it is the gift of God: not of works, lest any man should boast. For we are His workmanship, created in Christ Jesus unto

good works, which God has before ordained that we should walk in them.

There are many believers walking at a distance from the Lord today because God allowed or sent trouble their way. Are you a trophy with atrophy? So many believers are experiencing arrested development because they have not come to grips with the implications of the Word of God where it says, "Do you not know that your body is a temple of the Holy Spirit who is in you, whom you have from God, and that *you are not your own*? For *you have been bought* with a price: therefore, glorify God with your body" (1 Corinthians 6:19–20). If you fail to embrace these words with all of your heart, you run the very real risk of seeing your Christian development become characterized by atrophy—underdevelopment. When one considers the grace of God, spiritual atrophy is unreasonable. It is an unacceptable response to the grace and goodness of the Lord.

F. B. Meyer wrote, "Do we sufficiently realize the position into which the shedding of the blood of Jesus has brought us who believe? It is our ransom price, the purchase money of our entire being to be Christ's. The apostles lived in the days of a merciless form of slavery, but they never hesitated to borrow from it the imagery by which to set forth our relationship to our Savior. 'Not your own, but bought with a price.' 'Denying the Lord who bought them' (1 Corinthians 6:19–20; 7:23; 2 Peter 2:1). The purchaser of any slave regarded him as his chattel, his goods. He could, if he chose, fling him to feed his lampreys, and none might recompense or punish. He looked on all his belongings and earnings and talents as so many emoluments for himself. His word and will were absolute law. Such are the rights that our glorious Master has over us. He has redeemed us from the curse and penalty of sin to be a people for possession—HIS VERY OWN."[2]

According to 1 Corinthians 6:19–20, you do not have rights to your life. By that, I mean you do not have the right to choose what you will do with your life or the direction it should turn. You were created by Him and for Him (Colossians 1:16). Because you are not your own, you do not have a valid reason to complain or to become bitter about life. You do not have a life of your own. *You have been bought.* As a child of God, Jesus Christ holds the deed to your life, and thus the rights. Again, the Word of God says in 1 Peter 2:9, that we are a "people for God's own possession." I wonder how God feels about the possessed living as though not possessed, having no biblical grasp of the fact that they have no rights to their lives? Every follower of the Lord Jesus Christ needs to come to the beautiful place of surrender and take on the heart of a servant, although it costs everything. It is only right that He have the rights to our rights. As the redeemed of God, we do not have the right to retain our rights. Where do we get the idea that we deserve to have an easy, carefree, trouble-free life? Those who desire to have, and think they deserve to have, a life of ease, pleasure, and comforts also believe they are greater than their Master. Rather than ease, pleasure, and comfort, Jesus, our Master, experienced or encountered disease, displeasure, and discomfort everywhere He turned.

Recently, I was leading a conference and staying in a motel that was not very nice. The sign out front said motel but it was actually a "low-tel." My spirit was a little critical until I heard the Lord gently whisper, "It is better than what I ever had." I preached for a church recently that did not remunerate my efforts as they could or should have. My attitude was adjusted quickly when I heard that same voice saying, "It's more than I ever got, and it's My message." Recently, I flew to Argentina to lead a conference and was inwardly grumbling about the nine-hour flight, when I heard the Lord say, "If you were traveling as I traveled, it would take you nine months." It is very easy for us to forget that we are servants of the Most High God. Often, we forget that we have forfeited our rights. You can waste your time thinking you deserve to stay in a better place, or you can invest your time with humility. The difference comes when we halt the stinking way of thinking that facilitates arrogant and prideful thought patterns such as *I am worthy of more than this. I deserve more.* I once heard of a Christian music group that sent a list of stipulations to churches that booked their ministry. The list included the demand for bottled spring water on stage during the concert and for some name-brand sparkling water in their hotel rooms. Who do we think we are? More importantly, what does God think about us?

When one studies Philippians 2, one cannot help but become a little embarrassed at some of our attitudes and mindsets. Jesus Christ the Lord humbled Himself to die the humiliating and excruciating death of the cross. The Bible teaches us in verses 1–9 that He gave up everything that we would grasp to retain, and He embraced everything we would struggle to escape. He let go of everything we would grasp, and He grasped everything we would let go of. We make ourselves celebrities, though He made Himself a servant.

I want you to examine your heart under the microscope of God's Word in Philippians 2. The Bible reads in verses five through eight:

Let this mind be in you, which was also in Christ Jesus: Who, being in the form of God, thought it not robbery to be equal with God: but made himself of no reputation, and took upon him the form of a servant, and was made in the likeness of men: and being found in fashion as a man, he humbled himself, and became obedient unto death, even the death of the cross.

How does your mindset compare with His? Remember, you actually are not comparing apples to apples because He is God and you are not. If anyone ever had the right to retain control over His rights, it was Jesus the Lord. When one ponders the extent of His humiliation and self-abasement, how can there be any room left for us to live our lives in any other fashion? Where is humility in the church? These verses teach us that both His head (mind) and body were in submission to His Father's will. Jesus is the Head of the church, and we are His body. We are to allow Him to determine our thinking. Jesus' head was not the only part abiding submissively before the Father's will. Verse eight teaches us that He subjected His body to the cross. Never forget that we, the church, are the body of Christ. Jesus says in Luke 9:23, "If any man will come after Me, let him deny himself, and take up his cross daily, and follow Me." Did our Lord deny Himself? According to Philippians 2:6–7, Jesus relinquished His right to His eternal existence and manifest glory. His choice enabled Him to submit to the incarnation whereby He took on human flesh in Bethlehem.

Luke 9:23 teaches us to take up our cross daily. Not only did He take up His cross, He got on that cross at Calvary of His own volition. He gave up his life. He put his body on that cruel tree. Why are we, Christ's body, so reluctant to get on the cross? We cling to our rights and treat God as if He were here to make our lives happier and more convenient. Notice from Luke 9:23 the demands of the Lord Jesus Christ on our lives. He teaches that there must be a daily desire, daily denial, daily death, and daily discipleship. He states, "If anyone wishes to come after Me." A wish or will is a desire. The reason so many Christians are not living life as if they are God's possession is because they do not have the daily desire required to emulate the example of the Lord Jesus. They do not see themselves as His trophy of grace. They live with ignorance toward His will and goal for their lives. Our bitterness and disillusionment portrays the misguided desires we harbor and often cloak so very well. But God sees through the façade and is intent on bringing it to the surface so we know what He knows to be true of us. Our lives for God must begin with a daily desire to honor God, regardless of the circumstances in which we find ourselves. However, the desire is only the beginning.

The daily desire must translate into a daily denial of that which is contrary to His will for us. Whether it is an action, activity, attitude or ambition, God wants us to have the willingness to empty ourselves even before we see what it will cost us or where it might lead us. He wants our hearts and our trust. When I think of Abraham taking his only son Isaac up Mount Moriah to sacrifice Him at the Lord's command, I see Abraham revealing his desire for God and his denial of himself. He desired to come after God, to walk in the path He saw his Father walking. He denied his own paternal desires by showing a willingness to sacrifice one of the dearest things in his life—his only son.

Chapter 4

VENDING MACHINE BELIEVERS

When God saved me, I had a conviction of my sinful condition and understood that I needed the forgiveness of a holy God. But my salvation was motivated in part by a desire to have a better life. My life was a mess, and I knew Jesus Christ was the answer to my problems. Therefore, I came into my relationship with the Lord desirous to see Him straighten out my life. We need to remember it is not about us; it is about Him. We need His grace and salvation whether He ever blesses us beyond His divine, eternal forgiveness or not. Of course, He always does, but this must not be our focus. Too many people who claim to be in a relationship with God have a self-centered mindset and approach toward the Lord. It is not about Him making our little worlds better. It is about Him using us to make His world a better place. It is not about Jesus bringing us honor and glory, but about Him using us to bring honor and glory to Him! It is not about us prospering, but about His kingdom prospering.

Christians who have not reckoned themselves as God's possession have a certain propensity to treat God as if He were a vending machine. Have you ever sought to purchase a soda or snack from the machine that keeps your money? More than once, I have entered the correct change, made my selection and nothing came out. There have also been those times when I have entered the correct amount of money, made my selection and the machine gave me a product that I did not chose. In my younger years, it was not uncommon for me to display my aggravation toward a few vending machines. Those times usually occurred when I was really in a hurry or desperate for a quick fix. You might have the tendency to treat God as a machine. Yes, I have rocked a few vending machines in my time. If you are not careful, you can have similar displays toward God.

Do you realize we were created for God? God does not exist for us. We exist that we might be the objects of His love and affection. I have prayed many times, only to see God respond in a way I did not pray He would. God uses these moments to reveal our hearts. We encounter adversity and disappointments to purify, portray, or protect our character. Often, God desires to portray us—to expose to us and to those watching our lives—what He knows to be true about us. Sometimes He reveals what is positive and at other times the negative. Sometimes ungodliness is revealed and sometimes holiness; sometimes us, sometimes Him.

Has God ever answered your prayers in a way you did not pray He would? How about those times when you have entered the correct change of service, devotion, and zeal as a follower of Christ, only to see something you didn't want to come out of the machine? Have you ever gotten angry with the Lord? Have you ever obeyed God, only to see your life's circumstances seem to portray that you have been disobeying the Lord? Do you believe He exists for us? Are you a vending machine believer?

The Bible has some examples of vending machine believers. We find one such example in the Old Testament. Malachi 3:13 depicts the heart of mankind's carnality when God pronounced His wrath against their waywardness. God's people had been sinning against God, because in their minds, they had tried to serve God, but to no avail. Because they had not received from their Vender all they had desired, the people of God sidelined themselves in sin by withholding their tithes and offerings. God used the prophet Malachi to pronounce judgment upon Israel. Listen carefully to verses 13 and 14 as the people reveal the same excuse we often employ in response to our great heavenly Vender:

"Your words have been arrogant against Me," says the Lord. "Yet you say, 'How have we spoken against Thee?' You have said, 'It is vain to serve God; and what profit is it that we have kept His charge, and that we have walked in mourning before the Lord of Hosts?'"

Did you note their argument? "What profit is there?" They felt they had entered the correct change of service, devotion, and obedience. They had kept His charge and walked in mourning before the Lord. Because of their wrong motives and selfish ambitions, they wondered why they had even approached that machine. The children of God began to perceive their walk with God as meaningless (vain) since He had not responded in a manner commensurate with their desires in life.

Don't we have the tendency to think, "Those bad, Old Testament people. They were always treating God with such frivolity!" Honestly, haven't we all found this ungodly, vending machine mentality residing in our hearts from time to time? It is usually accompanied by discouragement, resentment, and envy. These people have difficulty rejoicing with others who are experiencing the blessings of the Lord. It affects our praying because the devil takes advantage of the situation, telling us to try another machine; this one doesn't work. The verbal witness begins to wane because, who wants to tell others to patronize a machine that is going to steal their money or disappoint them? Faith degenerates and devotion crumbles until the devil has the child of God sidelined, watching others score for the Son of God. They stand there thinking, I used to be out there, playing like that, but who wants to play for such a coach anyway? What does it matter?

I love the story in the book of Daniel concerning Shadrach, Meshach, and Abednego facing the fiery furnace. In Daniel 3, King Nebuchadnezer had commanded all of the people in the kingdom to disobey the Word of God and commence with idolatrous worship. The three Jewish men refused to conform to the whims of society and thrust aside the will of God. As they were twice threatened by the king to bow to his god, they resisted the intimidation of a fiery death in a blazing furnace. Nebuchadnezer asked them a telling question saying, "What god is there to save you?" As you read their answer, decide for yourself if they were vending machine believers: "Our God will save us. But *even if He doesn't*, we will not bow down."

I pray God will give us more warriors for Jesus Christ who are going to keep loving Him and serving Him regardless of whether He positively responds to their circumstances. God, give us more who will stay the course of Your Word and will do so regardless of the consequences. I want to be more like those three young Hebrews.

Have you noticed that the church of our Lord Jesus Christ has begun to treat God as if He were our servant? We are living in a day when the church is more focused on getting all she can out of God, rather than being concerned with how much He can get out of us! How did the servants become lords and the Lord become the servant? He is not our servant; we are His servants. Many will say they have not fallen into this manner of thinking, but their lives declare something else. Their bitterness and resentment are the tale-tell signs of their wayward theology. Their lack of resolve to keep their hands to the plow, though they keep meeting the resistance of stony circumstances, gives them away. Many don't sing the praises of God like they once did. They find it a struggle to consistently spend meaningful time with the Lord on a daily basis. They feel a little uncomfortable around those believers who are always on fire, speaking of the work of God in their lives. Their fervor isn't what it used to be. As did the Apostle Peter upon denying the Lord, they walk at a guilty distance as well.

If you did not grasp anything else from our study of Ephesians 2 in the last chapter, make sure you understand that your salvation is not something you did for God; it is something God did for you! It ought to preclude any inclination to have a vending machine mentality. Having received the gift of eternal life, God performed His work of grace in your heart. Salvation is not man looking for God; it is God looking for man! And why did God do this but to *show* the unsurpassed riches of His grace (Ephesians. 2:7)! He has reclaimed us from the world so we might proclaim to the world the awesome reality of who He is! Sometimes this proclamation is most readily heard by the world when it is voiced from the privileged platforms of adversity, difficulty, inconvenience, aggravation, and heartache. How do you view yourself? What is your view of God? Are you a vending machine believer?

JOB'S JOB

As I began writing this chapter, I did not think that it was coincidental (or humorous) that I accidentally deleted it as soon as I finished most of my initial entry. It was as if God were giving me a quick check-up regarding my personal embracement of the chapter's basic premise. There was a man, a godly man, named Job who had an assignment from God that few would desire. Job's job wasn't fair, and it did not seem to come from a loving boss. Long before Romans 8:28 was inspired and written, God had etched on his heart the principle that all things work together for good to those who love God and are called according to His purposes. Before Romans 12:1 was inspired by the Holy Spirit to be written, the Holy Spirit had inscribed the very principle in Job's heart. Job's worship of God was a "living sacrifice, holy and acceptable unto God."

Job entered the University of Adversity through strange circumstances—*He was doing everything right in the sight of God.* Often, we have a mind-set that adversity merely comes to those who are living outside God's will for their lives. Particularly in

American Christianity, we seem to hear from many charlatans through television ministries that God wants us to prosper. These hirelings want us to believe that God will always bless us with material and physical prosperity contingent upon one's individual walk and pursuit of God. May I ask a question? Could this same message be preached to Job? He had friends who tried. There are times when God chooses to do something else with our lives. What if God chooses to give us abundance, not in the material realm, but in the spiritual dominion? Let's consider the life of one such example—Job. Who was Job, and what was Job's job?

Job was a person of impeccable integrity. Job 1:1 describes him as "perfect and upright, and one that feared God, and eschewed evil." Job was a man of great spiritual piety and holiness. Job was not merely righteous from man's perspective, but from God's perspective as well! He was a blameless man of God. Also, Job was a blessed man. God gave him incredible, bountiful blessings. According to verses two and three, Job had many children, a sign of God's greatest blessing. Materialistically, Job was a very wealthy. He had over 11,000 livestock, which is indicative of the good hand of God. Job was a blameless and blessed man.

It would be comfortable if the story stopped there, but the story doesn't. Job was a hated man. Verses six through seven present a troubling scenario for the weak in faith and for those who have tried to make God their servant. Satan waged a war against Job. Job 1:6 states, "Now there was a day when the sons of God came to present themselves before the Lord, and Satan came also among them." There are many interpretations of this verse, but I understand it simply to be a picture of departed souls coming to worship and join in fellowship with their God. As they come to worship the Lord, Satan also comes to accuse them, before God, of their unworthiness to be in His presence. Herein we find another of the Bible's revealed mysteries. In His sovereignty, God allows the devil to have entry into heaven—even to approach the mighty throne of God.

How can heaven be heaven when Satan still has access? Heaven is heaven because God's will is done in totality. Our Lord Jesus prayed, "Thy will be done in earth, *as it is in heaven*" (Matthew 6:10). Nothing occurs in heaven except that which is in accordance with God's perfect script. As a student of God's Word, I believe in the sovereignty of God. Although I do not want to enrage my hyper-Calvinistic friends with this statement, God does have a permissive will. His permissive will exists in light of His sovereign will; therefore, God in His sovereignty allows us to go our own way. In heaven, God has a perfect will, and it is always accomplished.

However, there exists a permissive will as well. Do you recall the lament of our Lord Jesus Christ when He approached Jerusalem, getting ever so near to His cross? He exclaimed, "Oh Jerusalem, Jerusalem, you who kill the prophets, and stone them which are sent to you, how often I wanted to gather you together, even as a hen gathers her chickens under her wings, and *you would not let me*" (Matthew 23:37).

The Bible reveals another example, as the Lord Jesus taught in Nazareth and attempted to minister there. The Bible says, "And He could do no miracle there except that He laid His hands upon a few sick people and healed them. And He was going around wondering at their unbelief" (Mark 6:5–6). Our sovereign Lord Jesus permitted the unbelief of the people to preclude His miracle-working power.

How about the permissive will of God revealed in our Jesus' arrest and betrayal as recorded in Matthew 26? Judas brought the Roman cohort to the place where our Lord was surely to be found. As they approached Him to make the arrest, Peter intervened by drawing a sword and cutting off the right ear of the high priest's slave. Jesus revealed an ability to constrain the men and to restrain their evil wills when He said, "Or do you not think that I cannot appeal to my Father, and He will at once put at My disposal more than twelve legions of angels" (verse 53)?

So God has a permissive will and allows the devil to approach the throne of God to carry on his evil intentions. In Job 1, we see the reason the devil is called the devil. The word means accuser. The devil is portrayed in his diabolical role, accusing righteous Job of being unrighteous. Has it ever occurred to you that the devil usually will not tell you anything but what is false? Most accusations he makes are lies and emanate from untruths. When a child of God is living in sin, he lies to that individual, telling him his activity is acceptable in God's sight. When that same child of God is living uprightly before the Lord, the devil tries to convince him God is not pleased with him. Satan tries to cast doubts into his mind and heart about God's love and acceptance. As much as the Holy Spirit is our resident Counselor, the devil is our present (not resident) adversary. He exists to adversely impact our spirituality by accusing us. Thanks be unto God that "greater is He that is in you, than he that is in the world" (1 John 4:4).

God could have spared Daniel from the lion's den. The Lord could have precluded Shadrach, Meshach and Abednego from facing a fiery furnace. He could have prevented Paul and Silas from entering the doors of their Philippian prison. The apostle John found himself exiled on the island of Patmos. Sometimes the prerogative of God to allow His choice servants to suffer is difficult to reconcile in one's heart. It is, however, the prerogative of a sovereign God.

Why does He make the choice to send his best through the worst? Satan opposes God by opposing us. God opposes Satan by using us. Martin Luther said, "The devil is God's devil." I like to take the idea one uncomfortable step further and say, "The saints are God's saints." As God uses the devil for His own holy purposes, God uses us. Here, God uses Satan's accusation against Job to reveal truth. Satan's lies usually reveal truth. When he says something, find the antithesis, and you will usually find the truth. Remember this as you read Job 1:6–9:

> Now there was a day when the sons of God came to present themselves before the Lord, and Satan came also among them. And *the Lord said* unto Satan, Whence comest thou? Then Satan answered the Lord, and said, From going to and fro in the earth, and from walking up and down in it. And the Lord said unto Satan, Hast thou considered my servant Job, that there is none like him in the earth, a perfect and an upright man, one that feareth God, and escheweth evil? Then Satan answered the Lord, and said, Doth Job fear God for nought?

The devil, the great accuser of the brethren, is seen here in prime form. Being true to the meaning of his wicked name, Satan serves as Job's adversary by accusing him before the Lord of not being real. Make careful note of Satan's goal—opposing God. The instrument of his opposition is the child of God. The devil opposes God by opposing us. With all of the chaos in the world today, it seems as though Satan is winning the battle. I love what Erwin Lutzer wrote in *The Serpent of Paradise*, "The battle is never as close as God allows it to appear to be" (p. 80).[1]

If he had not been walking so closely with the Lord, Job might have felt like he was on the losing team.

These verses in Job reveal the devil opposing God by accusing God's choice servant of not being real. In other words, Satan is telling God, "Your work of grace in his life is a façade. Job's fidelity toward you is only based on the things you have done for him. He doesn't love You for who You are but for what You do for him. *He isn't in it for nothing.* Take away the blessings and You will strip away his affection and loyalty toward You."

Our worship of God is not acceptable until it is voluntarily offered for *who* God is. Think about Satan's simultaneous accusation toward God. He accused God of not being worthy of worship apart from His blessings. May I ask you a question? Why do you worship God with your words, songs, and obedience? What motivates your adoration of the Lord? Worship is not worship until it is offered from a heart that loves and respects God for who He is, rather than for the blessings He bestows on His children. We need to worship God because He is worthy of worship and has the profound right to be worshipped. The blessings I have received from the Lord since becoming His child merely extend and expand the breadth of my worship, but not the depth. The love He poured out for me at Calvary will fuel my adoration, praise, and surrender from now through all of eternity. I want to yield to Him because of Who He is, not merely for the blessing.

God wants our love for Him to be as His love is for us. Do you realize that God is in His relationship with you for nothing? God has nothing to gain from you. He is in His relationship with you for nothing. I do not want you to think God does not want something from you. God is totally sufficient in and of Himself. He has no needs, and certainly none you could meet. Do you believe God has needs that you can meet? Some believe they can glorify God. Others believe they can provide God with fellowship.

There is a doctrine in theological circles called the solitariness of God. No one articulates it better than Arthur Pink. In his book entitled, *The Attributes of God*, Pink describes this doctrine:

> "'In the beginning, God' (Genesis 1:1). There was a time, if 'time' it could be called, when God, in the unity of His nature (though subsisting equally in three Divine Persons), dwelt alone. 'In the beginning, God.' There was no heaven, where His glory is now particularly manifested. There was no earth to engage His attention. There were no angels to hymn His praises; no universe to be upheld by the word of His power. There was nothing, no one, but God; and that, not for a day, a year, or an age, but 'from everlasting.' During a past eternity, God was alone: self-contained, self-sufficient, self-satisfied; in need of nothing. Had a universe, had angels, had human beings been necessary to Him in any way, they also would have been called into existence from all eternity. The creating of them when He did, added nothing to God essentially. He changes not (Malachi 3:6); therefore His essential glory can be neither augmented nor diminished. God is no gainer even from our worship. He was in no need of that external glory which arises from His redeemed, for He is glorious enough in Himself without that.' "[2]

Think about the ramification of such a doctrine, that God has nothing to gain from us. He is totally self-sufficient and glorious without us. He doesn't need anything from you. He is no worse off, less God, or glorious without you. He is God, and God has no needs. Why did He create us and save us? Because

He wanted to! He did not need us—He wanted us. Therefore, since He has nothing to gain, *He is in it with us for nothing!*

I believe God wants you to meditate on that thought. He has nothing to gain from creating you and beginning a relationship with you. He has nothing to gain from you because He already has everything He could possibly need. If you could have added to Him, He would have called you into existence from eternity past. He is in His relationship with you for nothing, and that is what He wants us to reciprocate to Him. God does not love us for what we can give to Him. He does not love us because of what we can do for Him. He does not need anything! He loves you for who you are, not for the things you might do for Him.

God is in His relationship with us for nothing. He desires something from us, but He doesn't need anything. God is infinitely honorable and glorious, even if man or angel were never to honor or glorify Him again! He is sufficient in Himself. He always has been and always will be! C. S. Lewis wrote, "A man can no more diminish God's glory by refusing to worship Him than a lunatic can put out the sun by scribbling the word 'darkness' on the walls of his cell."[3] He does not need our worship, our love, or our companionship. He desires it because He deserves it. But if His desire goes unmet, He is not left in need. He is what He desires. He possesses what He deserves. If He had a need mankind could have met, we would have existed long before we did! God has nothing to gain from you, for He has always possessed that which you could give. God is in His relationship with you for nothing.

With these truths in view, ponder Satan's accusation toward Job. J. Dwight Pentecost summarized it well, "So Satan stood in front of God and insulted Him. He said to God, in effect,

'You bought Job with Your blessings; You bought his worship; You bought his obedience; he would be insane not to continue this ritual so that You would continue Your material blessings to him.'"[4] There is an inherent truth emanating from Satan's accusation. Satan asks God, "Does Job fear God for nothing?" I believe God is in the process of purifying our faith from the moment we are born again until we truly love Him for nothing. He wants us to love Him without regard for our personal gain. What spouse would not want to be loved except for who they are on the inside? Would you rather people love you for who you are or for what you do for them?

Please do not misunderstand me. There is no doubt that I love God more because of all He has done for me through salvation. Jesus said that some would love more because they have been forgiven of more (Luke 7:47). If it were not for the things He has done, I would not know God. But I believe God wants to get us to the place where we remain steadfast and true, regardless of another blessing or another answered prayer. I would hope that my wife would continue in faithful relationship with me, even if the day were to come that I am physically incapacitated and totally useless for meeting most of her needs. What if God were suddenly rendered unable to guide the events of your life with victorious or glorious results? That is a sobering question. Read it again, and think about it. Are you in it for nothing?

Job's life took a sudden, harsh turn. The terrorists' attacks on the World Trade Center on September 11, 2001, give an added meaning to the cliché "in a New York minute." It is amazing how quickly life changed for all of us that day. With such rapidity, Job saw his life change! In a brief span of time, his life would never be the same. His problems are difficult for me to fathom:

And there came a messenger unto Job and said, The oxen were plowing, and the asses feeding beside them: And the Sabeans fell upon them, and took them away; yea, they have slain the servants with the edge of the sword; and I only am escaped to tell thee. While he was yet speaking, there came also another, and said, The fire of God is fallen from heaven, and hath burned up the sheep, and the servants, and consumed them; and I only am escaped alone to tell thee. While he was yet speaking, there came also another, and said, Thy sons and thy daughters were eating and drinking wine in their oldest brother's house; and, behold, there came a great wind from the wilderness, and smote the four corners of the house, and it fell upon the young men, and they are dead; and I only am escaped to tell thee." (Job 1:14–19)

So went Satan forth from the presence of the Lord, and smote Job with sores from the sole of his foot unto his crown." (Job 2:7)

Life can be so unfair. Solomon said, "I have seen everything during my lifetime of futility; there is a righteous man who perishes in his righteousness, and there is a wicked man who prolongs his life in wickedness' (Ecclesiastes 7:15, New American Standard Version). As a result of Satan's accusation, God allowed a series of problems for Job to encounter. Job's job was to prove the devil to be the liar he is. Satan accused Job of being faithful in his relationship with God because of the gain of personal blessings. He accused him of selfish motives. He accused Job of being evil. He accused God of not being good enough. Satan's accusations toward man are always a simultaneous, subtle attack against God. In accusing Job, Satan indicted that God was a failure in producing a trophy of grace. Satan wants to use us to show that God produces people of façade rather than people of faith. The Bible teaches, "For we are His workmanship, created in Christ Jesus unto good works" (Ephesians 2:10). Ultimately, Satan is telling God He is a failure in His spiritual creativity.

How many times has this heavenly scenario occurred with a slightly different slant? How about the times Satan has waged the same accusation with your name rather than Job's? I think the average follower of Jesus Christ is totally ignorant of the heavenly drama often being played before his or her eyes. Never forget that Satan did not call for Job; God called for Satan to consider Job! It is God's right and prerogative.

How many times are we ignorant of the reason behind our times of aggravation, distress and discomfort? Every episode of ungodliness in our lives is an affirmation of the devil's accusations. Our bitterness and unfaithfulness affirm Satan's lies. Or, how often is he correct? I wonder how often you respond to the trials and little setbacks in life in a manner that you enable the devil to look at God and say, "I told you so. Look at him. There goes that spiritual roller coaster you call a trophy of grace."

As the winds of adversity blew against his family, body and possessions, Job's heart revealed a perspective few would expect. Job was real. Not perfect, but real. Listen to his perspective:

Then Job arose, and rent his mantle, and shaved his head, and fell down upon the ground and worshipped, and said, Naked came I from my mother's womb, and naked shall I return thither: the Lord gave, and the Lord hath taken away; blessed be the name of the Lord." (Job 1:21–22)

Shall we receive good at the hand of God, and shall we not receive evil. (2:10)

Though he slay me, yet will I trust in him. (13:15)

God wants to produce children who are consistent and steadfast. "Be steadfast, immovable, always abounding in the work of the Lord" (1 Corinthians 15:58, New American Standard). He is looking for those who would rather have Him with trials than to have no trials without Him! Personally, I would rather have God with me in a life of trials than to have a life without God and no trials. You will never get to the point of being in it for nothing until God allows trials and disappointments in your life to purify your faith. If you never grow beyond an *in it for something* faith, what will happen to your walk with God if He decides to take you down a similar path Job traveled? Why are you in your personal relationship with God? Are you in it for nothing?

There have been times in my life when I have been sick and tired. There have also been times when I have been sick and tired of being sick and tired. There have been times when I have been sick and tired of being sick and tired of being sick and tired. Can you empathize with that? We must live our lives for the glory of God. In order to do so, we must relinquish any demands or expectations to have a life free from adversity. If you want a life where frustration and difficulty are foreign to your experience, you are in it for something. If you want a life as a Christian that is easy and comfortable, then you have a loftier standard for your life than did the Son of God.

Aren't you glad the Lord Jesus Christ accepted the plan of servitude? Jesus' choice led Him down a road never traveled where He ended up on a hill called Calvary. There, the sinless Son of God encountered something He had never known before—sin. He became sin for us. Has it ever occurred to you that nails did not hold Him on the cross? It was a desire He demonstrates and exemplifies for every individual who would desire to be a servant of God. He was in it for nothing but the

glory of His Father. If glorifying His Father meant the acceptance of unjust accusations, then so be it. If honoring His Father meant unjustly suffering at the hands of guilty sinners, then
so be it. If magnifying His Father meant enduring the shame of
the cross, then so be it. He was not living his life for selfish gain
or the pursuit of a personal agenda. The Lord Jesus humbled
Himself even to the point of death—even death on a cross. He
did it for us.

Surely, there have been times when Satan has questioned
God's integrity as a master builder. I know this to be true because of the difficulties that have come into my life over the
years. I am certain the devil has touched the affairs of my life in
pursuit of slandering God's integrity as a spiritual builder. God
is the architect and builder of my spiritual pilgrimage. Sometimes life can be full of adversity and heartaches. More often
than we realize, the devil is trying to tarnish God's character
and to destroy God's children. I chose to live my life cognizant
of this demonic activity in order to prove the devil a deceiver.
Sometimes, I wonder why God does not spread out these opportunities among the brethren more thinly. I choose to believe
that He is entrusting me with these precious opportunities to
prove Him as worthy. I want to affirm the worthiness of God,
not the worthiness of what He has done for me. It was Job's job.
It is my job. It is your job.

Because of his faithful response, God graciously blessed Job
with double for his trouble. Job succeeded at his job. He honored God. Yes, the book of Job reveals a man, human to the
core with frailty and questions. In light of his compassionless
counselors called friends, I am surprised he did not struggle
more. God welcomes our prayerful dialogue. We have a relationship with Him. We have fellowship with Him. Our dialogue does not have to be right. God knows our hearts, and He

loves us. He welcomes the expression of our feelings and our complaints. He wants our fellowship. Job was real. His faithful response to his trials concluded with a heavenly vindication. God gave Job twice as much livestock as he had before (Job 42:10). God replaced his seven sons and three daughters. How sweet it must have been for Job to once again hear the cry of babies in the night. What pleasure it must have given for him to look out the window of his home and watch 14,000 sheep grazing green pastures where the fire of God once incinerated his entire herd. Because he responded uprightly to his adversity, God gave Job double for his trouble!

Job found himself basking in the sweet victory of God's merciful and victorious vindication. On a personal note, I can testify to the sweet reality that God gives double for your trouble. After our daughter died, I felt the joy of His vindication when Baxter was born 16 months later. I felt it again when Jackson was born 18 months later. I felt it again when Carson was born 28 months later. I want you to be assured that God will vindicate your circumstances. One way or another, you will receive from the Lord in such a manner that you will be glad you encountered your difficulties. Truly, you will be thankful for all things (Ephesians 5:20). If you respond correctly, someday you will embrace the adversities of your life as a dear friend. The prerequisite—a proper response!

I would not be as far along in my walk with God if it were not for the trials God has allowed to touch my life. I am more useable, and if that were the only outcome of my time at the University of Adversity, it would still be worth it! Is not the purpose of an education to be more useable? Job was a useable man. After so many centuries, just think of the way God still uses him. Every time God enrolls me in another class at the University of Adversity, I reflect on the lives of Job and the Lord Jesus Christ.

Chapter 6

LIVING IN LIGHT OF OTHERS

Heaven is only one place where the devil accuses us. The Word of God reveals three stages where he acts out his slanderous script. Revelation 12:10–11 says, "The accuser of the brethren is cast down, which accused them before our God day and night. And they overcame him by the blood of the Lamb, and by the word of their testimony; and they loved not their lives unto death." Clearly, these verses reveal a heavenly accusation. As we learned from Job, this activity occurs before the very throne of God. However, there will come a day when Satan will be stripped forever of his God-given ability to engage God in heaven. These verses in Revelation foretell of his certain excommunication from heaven. For the time being, we must understand that the devil accuses us in the heavens.

The devil also seeks to accuse us in our hearts. Spiritual warfare is a reality usually played out in our hearts and minds. The devil accuses us of not being genuinely saved. He wants us to believe we are not really accepted by God. He accuses us of being too ungodly to be the children of God. The devil accuses us of having wrong motives when we have the correct motives. He injects us with feelings of guilt, even when we have done nothing to be guilty of. When difficulties come, he tries to convince us we must not really be saved. Satan attempts to convince us that God is not happy with us.

Spiritual warfare involves the spiritual armor God provides every child of God. It is described partially in Ephesians 6:14 as "the breastplate of righteousness." A military soldier in the apostle Paul's day protected his heart and other vital organs with a breastplate. As the devil accuses us in our hearts, we have adequate protection with the righteousness of God. Every word of accusation the devil conjures up regarding me or my salvation can be thwarted by the donning of the breastplate of righteousness, whereby I agree with the Word of God—that I am who God says I am. Revelation 12:11 proclaims, "They overcame him by the blood of the Lamb, and by the word of their testimony." When a Christian knows he has been saved according to the promises of the Word of God, thus giving him a personal testimony, he possesses an immense fortress of protection surrounding his heart. The child of God is able to withstand the demonic assaults on the heart when living in agreement with the promises of imputed righteousness and by living a holy life in agreement with that testimony. There must be no hypocrisy in our lives if we are going to benefit from the breastplate of righteousness. Your lifestyle must match your testimony. The imputed and imparted righteousness of God is our breastplate, and it is sufficient for protecting our hearts during Satan's diabolical assaults.

The devil also accuses us before humanity. Take careful note of Revelation 12:11 when it says, "They loved not their own lives unto death." How did these believers, during the tribulation, get to the place of giving their very lives for their faith in

Jesus Christ? They were accused among humanity of not being real. The devil lies to lost people about the validity of our faith. Yes, Satan accuses us in the heavens, in our hearts, and before humanity. He tells God we are not real. He attempts to convince our hearts we are not real. He tries to convince others we are not real. These precious saints in the tribulation will be accused by the devil of not being genuine, and God will give them the blessed privilege and honor of affirming Him again as the master builder of human hearts. These precious saints will be set on the mantle of God's glory as trophies of grace to serve as eternal reminders of His goodness and power! Some saints are being given this privilege in our world today.

Think about this principle activity Satan employs in our lives. Most of us will never have the privilege to die for the testimony of Jesus Christ, but do you realize God gives us opportunities to stand for Him at many other times. The context of our opportunities might not seem as drastic as the tribulation saints will endure; nonetheless they are extremely important as Satan accuses us before humanity. He seeks to convince the people watching our lives that we are not what we claim to be. He wants to see us contradict our testimonies by improperly responding to life's dilemmas and trials. Satan wants people to see us ride a spiritual roller coaster of inconsistency so they will not desire the Christian life we claim to be so wonderful and fulfilling.

Every child of God should enjoy the freeing power of their acceptance and reconciliation with God to the degree they feel welcomed by God to be real in the expression of their emotions, feelings, and doubts. We have a relationship with God, and to squelch or suppress the expression of our humanness and frailty is acceptable with God. The Psalms are full of the thoughts of a man after God's own heart expressing the reality of his concerns, frustrations, and doubts. God wants us to be real. I do not believe He wants us to live behind a carnal façade of optimism that we hope others perceive as faith. I think it is best to hash out these personal struggles of faith and weakness in my times of personal devotion and meditation. The Lord Jesus left His disciples some distance away, and He went to the rock at Gethsemane alone with his Father to lay his issues to rest.

Perhaps you are going through a tough time right now. How does God want you to live? How are you to respond to the very real challenges and heartaches you are facing? As you are being honest with God about your struggles, complaints, and concerns, God wants you to live your life in light of others. The apostle Paul did not live a life devoid of hardships and adversity. Actually, the Bible reveals a man who encountered difficulty because he was doing the will of God! As the drama in a great missionary's life unfolds in Acts 16, the Word of God gives a subtle and crucial example of our need to live in light of those who inevitably observe our lives.

"And the multitude rose up together against them: and the magistrates rent off their clothes, and commanded to beat them. And when they had laid many stripes upon them, they cast them into prison, charging the jailor to keep them safely: who, having received such a charge, thrust them into the inner prison, and made their feet fast in the stocks. And at midnight, Paul and Silas prayed, and sang praises unto god: *and the prisoners heard them.* And suddenly there was a great earthquake, so that the foundations of the prison were shaken: and immediately all the doors were opened, and every one's bands were loosed. And the keeper of the prison awaking out of his sleep, and seeing the prison doors open, he drew out his sword, and would have killed himself, supposing that the prisoners had been fled. But Paul cried with

a loud voice, saying, 'Do thyself no harm: for we are all here.'
Then he called for a light, and sprang in, and came trem-
bling, and fell down before Paul and Silas, and brought them
out, and said, 'Sirs, what must I do to be saved?' And they
said, 'Believe on the Lord Jesus Christ, and thou shalt be
saved, and thy house.' And they spoke unto him the word of
the Lord, and to all that were in his house. And he took them
the same hour of the night, and washed their stripes, and was
baptized, he and all his, straightway. And when he had
brought them into his house, he set meat before them, and
rejoiced, believing in God with all his house. And when it
was day, the magistrates sent the serjeants, saying, 'Let those
men go.'" (Acts 16:22–35).

I think we are reading about two men of God who were in
it for nothing! Paul and Silas were in a stormy circumstance as a
result of doing what they were supposed to be doing. Somehow,
that doesn't seem fair, does it? But, through the darkness of their
midnight hour and through their proper response, Paul and Silas
display the worthiness of God! Then, God put on a display!
Paul and Silas were set free in an unorthodox manner. The jailer
charged to keep them in prison became the one who led them
out. The jailor led them out and into his very home. The one
who previously guarded against their escaping now gave them
food in his home. He nursed the wounds his colleagues inflicted.
Most importantly, he and his family accepted the gospel message that Paul and Silas came preaching in the first place. The
impact of the earthquake God used to free Paul and Silas was
extensive. Paul and Silas were two men who were in it for nothing. They were living in light of others.

We have already considered another story with a similar
application. Let's refresh our memories from the narrative of
Jesus asleep in the boat.

"And the same day, when the even was come, he saith unto them, 'Let us pass unto the other side.' And when they had sent the multitude away, they took him even as he was in the ship. And there were also with him *other little ships*. And there arose a great storm of wind, and the waves beat into the ship, so that it was now full. And he was in the hinder part of the ship, asleep on a pillow: and they awake him, and say unto Him, 'Master, carest thou not that we perish?' And He arose, and rebuked the wind, and said unto the sea, 'Peace, be still.' And the wind ceased, and there was a great calm. And He said unto them, 'Why are ye so fearful? How is it that ye have no faith?'" (Mark 4:35–40).

Go back and study these two accounts. Take particular note of the markedly different responses of Jesus' disciples in the grips of difficult circumstances. These are the two ways you can respond to every trial that touches your life. You can look to God in fear, or you can look to Him in faith! You can live in fear or live by faith. Through their imprisonment, Paul and Silas chose the look of faith. In the storm, the disciples chose the look of fear. If you are going to live in light of the little boats and prisoners in your life, you must not neglect the look of faith. The crucial thing is whether my response to adversity will leave people watching my life more desirous to know Jesus. We are good at talking about him when things are going smoothly, but how good are we at trusting him when things get a little rough?

Just like Paul and Silas, there are always going to be people observing our lives. Often, they are prisoners as well. They are people enslaved to sin having never trusted the shackle-shattering power of Jesus Christ to free them from the chains of sin. How about the people watching your life from those little boats? Do not forget the vast difference between their circumstances and the disciples on that stormy night. Contrary to the little boats, the twelve disciples had the Lord Jesus Christ in their boat. If anyone had a reason for calm, it was the passengers in the boat with the Master of the sea. I doubt their fearful response to the storm gave those in the little boats much desire to receive Christ into the boats of their hearts. The disciples failed to respond in such a manner that the others could readily see the positive effect of having Jesus in their boat. I do not ever want to lose my focus of faith in the trials of life whereby I fail to live in light of the spiritual needs of those watching my life. Who are the prisoners, jailors, and mariners watching your life? If you never realize another reason for your trials, understand they are for the glory of God. The question is this—will my life make others hungry to know Jesus Christ! Is God using your life to awaken in others their need for a relationship with Jesus? It is not easy, but it is possible through the Holy Spirit!

I will never forget a pastor's wife who attended our daughter's funeral. Darlene has always had a very talkative, outgoing personality. I had joined her husband numerous times over the years in praying for her salvation. After the funeral, I mentioned to my wife that something seemed wrong with Darlene that day. Granted, the atmosphere was not light. However, I had not seen much that would dampen her wonderful, spirited personality. Two weeks after the funeral, our phone rang. On the other end of the line was Darlene crying and attempting to share how she had received Jesus that morning at church. She told me that she watched Lisa and me at Leah's funeral. She knew if she were going through our circumstances she would not be able to respond in the same manner. She realized the problem in her life was the result of lacking a personal relationship with Jesus Christ. Her husband led her to a saving faith in Jesus that morning! Pastor's wives make better pastor's wives when they are saved. Do you know for certain that you have a personal relationship with God through Jesus Christ?

One of the joys I had as a pastor was leading the church to embrace foreign missions. We took our first trip overseas to Argentina, where I had the privilege of sharing my testimony one morning as I preached the gospel. I will never forget that Argentine church planter telling me of a pastor who needed to hear my story. He scheduled a time for me to visit with Pastor Jorge and his wife Miriam. The day before our meeting, our church canvassed the community near Jorge's house seeking to share the gospel. We approached a home where a young woman in her thirties was seated in the doorway holding a baby. She looked up at us, stood to her feet and walked away. As we turned to leave, our translator alerted us that she had returned. I began to tell her we were in the neighborhood sharing with people how they can know they have eternal life. She responded saying, "I used to believe, but a year ago my daughter died. I do not understand how God is good and could let my daughter die." I told her, "I had a daughter who died, and I still think God is good."

We answered as many of Maria Rosa's questions as possible as we shared the Word of God. She eventually received Jesus Christ as her personal Lord and Savior. The next day I met with Jorge and Miriam. My heart broke as they shared their heart-wrenching story. It is so reminiscent of my own testimony. They started a church in their home, and Miriam gave birth to a daughter. When the baby was ten months old, they discovered the baby in her crib not breathing. They were able to rouse her back to consciousness and get her in their car. Unfortunately, halfway to the hospital, their car broke down. Jorge and Miriam began running up the highway carrying their daughter the rest of the way. The baby died in Miriam's arms on the side of the road of Sudden Infant Death Syndrome. It is interesting that God had me visiting a country nearly 5500 miles away, only to meet a pastor with a similar testimony. Both of us were married and had one child when we started churches in our homes. Our wives became pregnant as we started the churches. Both of us had daughters. Our daughters died in our wives arms before their first birthdays. Both of us had broken hearts.

Because I had been in a boat similar to theirs, God gave me the ability to minister the Word of God in a helpful way. I was able to comfort them with the comfort I had received in Christ Jesus (2 Corinthians 1). After God ministered to their needs and set them on the road to healing, they were able to assimilate Maria Rosa into their church. I preached for their congregation a year later and there was Maria Rosa on the front row with a friend she invited. Maria is in a church with a pastor and wife who can empathize and sympathize with her pain. If you will live in light of others, you will be given the most fulfilling opportunities to see your trials used for the furtherance of God's kingdom and for the mending of broken hearts.

Have you ever thought about the difference between a marble and a grape when you crush them? When enough pressure is exerted on a marble, dangerous fragments of glass propel outward. Exert pressure on a grape, and you might produce a fine wine. One obvious difference between these dissimilar objects is their softness. If your heart becomes hard and bitter through life's trials, you will probably hurt those around you like the sharp glass. How do you respond to the pressures of life? Is your heart soft before God? Are you submissive?

I have heard people say, "Don't forget in the darkness what God has shown you in the light." I would like to add to that, "Don't forget in the light what God has shown you in the darkness." The things we learn from better and bitter times of life are invaluable truths. They are the principles we need to grasp for our lives and for the sake of helping others. Are you living in light of others?

I want to close this chapter with a simple poem God led me to write:

When God in His sovereignty your heart He breaks,
Don't forget in the darkness He causes earthquakes!
So in how you respond, don't make a mistake.
Remember the jailor; that souls are at stake.
Like Job you must say, 'God can give and can take.'
According to His Word He's working good for my sake.
Your faith will be tested, proven real or perhaps fake.
But whatever He shows you, let Him a soldier make.

Chapter 7

LUI: LIVING UNDER THE INFLUENCE

"... be ye filled with the Holy Spirit." (Ephesians 5:18)

As I am writing these words, God is reminding me of my inability to live these truths. I do not like to be in it for nothing. Sometimes I get to that point in my heart, but to stay there is another challenge. My responsibility in the Christian life is to die to myself and seek to be obedient to the Word of God. I am to yield and surrender to the Lord. My responsibility is not to exude the fruit of the Spirit but to allow the Holy Spirit to bear it on the limbs of my life.

For the first several years of my Christian walk, I lived with the wrong assumption that God saves us, and it is our responsibility to take the reins from that point and live for God. But the Bible says, "As ye have therefore received Christ Jesus as Lord, so walk in Him" (Colossians 2:6). How did we receive Christ as Lord except by "grace through faith" (Ephesians 2:8)? Hence, if we are to "so walk in Him," we must live the Christian life by grace through faith. In other words, we are saved by His grace through faith, and we live the Christian life by His grace through faith. The Christian life is God doing something for us (grace) that we are powerless to do ourselves. Faith is the way of living the Christian life. We trust Him to save us and to live His life through us. God does not want you to make up your mind to start doing better. He wants much more than that.

God taught me these truths again when He called me to preach revival meetings for a rural church in another state. It was one of those churches so far removed from civilization that I was not sure God even knew where it was located. Because the music was so bad and the church was so dead, I could hardly stand before the people to preach. I did the best I could to conjure up some enthusiasm. Somehow, I got through it.

When I returned to the motel that afternoon, I wrestled with the Lord about going home. I just wanted to pack my things, load my car, and go home. I called my wife, and she told me I had to stay. Then, I took up my argument with the Lord. I said, "God, it is so bad." He replied, "That is why you are here." I said, "But it is awful." Again, He said, "That is why you are here." I got frustrated and said, "I can't do it." He quickly replied, "That's why *I'm* here." At that point, I thought God was finished with the conversation. Not long after He spoke those enlightening words, I was feeling a little better. Suddenly, He said, "You couldn't do it even if it were good." After I got my heart right, God really began to bless the ministry through the week. I have preached for the same church on three different occasions since.

Think about the lesson God was teaching me. He was reminding me that I need Him all the time, just the same, in every circumstance. God did not save me and call me to serve Him in my own strength. He did not send me to that dead church leaving it up to me to conjure what they needed in my flesh or carnal ingenuity. God does not want you to face the challenges of life with some carnal concoction of joy and peace. He does not want you to tackle life with carnal concoctions of courage or feeble façades of fleshly fortitude.

Do you understand what He was teaching me? Meditate upon it. God will not call you to do something and then expect you to accomplish it in your own strength. God wants you to experience the fruit of the Holy Spirit recognizable by a life of "love, joy, peace, patience, kindness, goodness, faithfulness, gentleness, and self-control" (Galatians 5:22 New American Standard Bible). God wants to live His life through us. He does not want us to *act* joyous; He wants us to *be* joyous! He does not want you to act loving; He wants to love through you!

I heard Elvis Presley being interviewed at a press conference when he was asked, "What do you think about your image as a shy, humble, country boy?" He replied, "Well, I'll tell you this. An image is a hard thing to live up to." I agree. And in the Christian realm, I believe it is impossible. The inconsistency of an individual trying to live like a Christian is personally frustrating and it is confusing to the lost. Aren't you glad God has not called you to paint a façade of godliness with your fleshly, human effort?

When God saved you, He did not take away your ability to live like you used to live before salvation. He has given you a new nature, but God did not eradicate your flesh. According to Romans 7, all of us still retain the ability to live according to the flesh. I heard a story about a pastor in a small town who had a rough weekend of ministry. When he arrived at the church on Monday morning, there was a dead mule in front of the main entrance to the building. He was pretty aggravated. He sat in his car and huffed and puffed before going inside to call the police. After they investigated the situation, they told the pastor there was nothing they could do since there was no apparent foul play. They recommended he call the health department. He huffed and puffed a while and reported the situation to the health department. They investigated the scene and told the pastor there was nothing they could do since the animal was not posing a health threat to the community. They suggested he call the sanitation department. Well, the pastor huffed and puffed a while and finally made the call. The sanitation manager told the pastor they did not have the authority to make such a pickup without prior approval from the city mayor. The pastor had a personal knowledge of the mayor's short temper. He thought about it a while and made the call. As he was describing the affair, the mayor interrupted the pastor and said, "Why are you calling me? It's your job to bury the dead." The pastor paused and retorted, "Yes, and it's my job to notify the next of kin, so I thought I would call and let you know." And the pastor slammed the phone down.

Even as the children of God, we have the ability to speak unkindly. We still have the propensity to act like we used to act before Jesus saved us. Too many of God's children are trying to live for Him and to act like Him. He does not want you to act like Him; God wants to be Himself in and through you. One of the most freeing times I have experienced was the day I began coming to grips with the fact that God does not want me to live for Him but to die to myself. You are called to take up your cross, a symbol of death (Luke 9:23). We are called to be living sacrifices, an assumption of death (Romans 12:1). We are called, moment by moment, to deny our personal attractions, ambitions, agendas, abilities, and affections. This is the road to the Spirit-filled life.

Anytime a child of God abandons control of his life, he is simultaneously filled with the Holy Spirit. To be filled with the Holy Spirit is to be controlled by the Holy Spirit. Ephesians 5:18 compares the Spirit-filled life with being physically drunk with an alcoholic beverage. If you make the comparison, it is easy to see the Spirit-filled life as an individual being controlled by a substance not of oneself. The Holy Spirit is the "beverage" we took in at salvation, and we are to give ourselves over to Him to the extent that He intoxicates (controls) us! Too many Christians are living sober lives. Are you so living under the control of God's Spirit that you could be found guilty of LUI: living under the influence? Drunkenness causes one to do things he or she normally would not do!

When I think about the times of adversity I have faced in life, God has often used these moments to show me how soberly I was living. Don't misunderstand me. As we await the second coming of our Lord, we are to be sober as we watch, wait, and serve Him. It is not uncommon for the Bible to present two ideas that seem in conflict with one another. We are to be sober as we seek to avoid the snares of the devil and intoxicated as we walk in cadence with the will of God. You will never pass the tests at the University of Adversity until you grasp the implication and application of the Spirit-controlled life. Unless controlled by His Spirit, you will never make the prisoners hungry to know our God. Except intoxicated by the Holy Spirit, you will never be used by God to show the little boats the difference Jesus Christ could make in their boats!

I am challenged every time I read verses similar to Ephesians 5:20 that teach, "Giving thanks always for all things." Does God really expect us to be thankful for all things always? I don't know about you, but I have trouble with this verse. It is not normal for me to have such an attitude of gratitude. Let's reconsider the idea of being filled with the Holy Spirit. The idea is that of being controlled by His Spirit. A drunken individual will do things he normally would not do. Therefore, I will respond to life in an uncommon fashion and in a manner foreign to my natural tendencies. When you are filled with the Holy Spirit, people will see such a difference in your personality, they might think you are having mental problems. How many people do you know who are thankful all of the time? How many people do you know who are thankful for all things all of the time?

I have shared with you about a few of the classes Lisa and I have attended at the University of Adversity. As we encountered those difficulties, there were some well-meaning saints in our congregations who had it in their power to minister to the needs we had in our lives, but lacked the sensitivity to act upon them. We had ample opportunities to become bitter toward those who could have made life a little easier for us. I have learned God will always see that you have ample opportunities to check your sobriety. He will leave just enough insensitive or cantankerous people in your life to keep you vigilant. God will see to it that you have enough of the wrong kind of people in your life to enable you to keep a thumb on the pulse of your spiritual inebriation.

God knows when we need a reality check, and He will provide the tests through perfectly timed periods of frustration, neglect, uncertainty, or heartache. These times in our lives reveal where we are with the Lord and where we are not. No matter how unjust or unfair the circumstances, we must not forget that we are not our own. We have been bought with the price of Jesus' blood. When our rights have been violated, we must remember we have no rights as servants of the King. We gave them up, just as He did. I do not mean civil rights but the right to determine what we are going to do and be in life. You are not your own, and you are not *on* your own! You have the Holy Spirit residing within to respond to life for you and through you! I have heard Dr. Adrian Rogers say, "Every Christian has the Holy Spirit resident, but not every Christian has Him as president." Allow the One residing inside you to preside as Lord over the affairs of your life! Give Him His rightful place of control.

Have you ever gone through a series of events when seemingly God would not give you a break? When you encounter these seasons of life, remember the opportunity and platform being given by God to respond in an uncommon fashion. If others in your life see you praising God, even in the darkness of your midnight hour, they just might realize their need of Him as well!

I chose to see the difficulties of life as opportunities to magnify the Lord Jesus Christ. What does it mean to magnify something, but to gain the advantage of a close view? As one looks through a magnifying glass to more easily see an object, so we enable those around us to more easily see the details of our awesome God. We magnify Him when we respond in a manner whereby people are enabled to perceive more of Him than they could otherwise see with the naked eye of normal circumstances.

There is a way to love people who have wronged you. God is able to provide all you need to love them and not reciprocate your actions. There is a way to have joy regardless of outward circumstances or future prospects for relief. There is a way to experience real peace in the face of great uncertainty. There is peace available despite the storms of life. Kind words and deeds are more than possible even when you have been treated unkindly. There is the ability to remain faithful and true to God even in the tempests of mental, spiritual, and physical anguish.

God gives us the ability to obey Him. He gives us all we need to be what He calls us to be. This principle is well illustrated in Exodus 16:22–30, when God calls the Israelites to rest on the Sabbath:

"Now it came about on the sixth day they gathered twice as much bread, two omers for each one. When all the leaders of the congregation came and told Moses, then he said to them, 'This is what the Lord meant: Tomorrow is a Sabbath observance, a holy Sabbath to the Lord. Bake what you will bake and boil what you will boil. And all that is left over put aside to be kept until morning.' So they put aside until morning, as Moses had ordered, and it did not become foul, nor was there any worm in it. And Moses said, 'Eat it today, for today is a Sabbath to the Lord; today you will not find it in the field. Six days you shall gather it, but on the seventh day, the Sabbath, there will be none.' And it came about on the seventh day that some of the people went out to gather, but they found none. Then the Lord said to Moses, 'How long do you refuse to keep My commandments and My instructions? See, the Lord has given you the Sabbath; therefore He gives you bread for two days on the sixth day' (New American Standard).

The Lord gave them all they needed ahead of time in order to obey His demands! He does the same for us no matter what dilemma we encounter. He calls for holiness in hellish times, and He supplies bread ahead of time to meet His demand for love, kindness, patience, and joy in our lives! God does not expect you to endure the challenges of life by the frustrating and futile fortitude of your flesh. God does not expect you to produce the proper Christian response to the strife of life. The choice you make will be the difference between contriving the Christian life and thriving in the Christian life. It will mean the difference between merely surviving and thriving! The fruit of the

Spirit is available for the controlled saint of God—for the one who is Spirit-filled! The Spirit-filled life is a choice we make, moment by moment, to depend on God's grace.

Are you LUI? Are you living a life of holiness before God? Are you being disobedient to Him in any area of your life? Are you dying daily to self? Are you depending upon the Holy Spirit to live the life of Jesus Christ through you? Are you consistent? LUI: it is the only way.

LIVING IN THE LAND OF "NO CAN DO"

"... when I am weak, then I am strong." (2 Corinthians 12)

I attended a church service once when a young group of elementary and middle school students were asked to play their instruments for the special music during the worship service. As they were introduced, I could not help but notice that a few of the adult members of the church orchestra came and joined the group of young musicians. I assume they were participating to fill in some empty parts in the repertoire that evening. The young musicians gave an excellent performance and did the best they could with their experience, skills, and abilities. Even though they had the adults reinforcing their efforts, it was apparent they would not be playing for a major symphony anytime soon. Their combined effort was not exactly pleasing to the ear, but it was a good idea to allow the young musicians the chance to participate in ministry. It did cross my mind during their performance that it would have sounded better if they had allowed the adults alone to play.

Isn't that the way it is when we live the Christian life through our own efforts while asking God to help us? The best music is played when we rest the instruments of our efforts and allow God the Holy Spirit to do what only He can do—play the music. God does not want us to live for Him in our own strength, all the while asking Him to merely fill in for where we fall short. The greatest chance God has to receive glory from our lives is when we are helpless and at the end of our ropes. He is desirous to see us get to the place of total dependence and reliance upon Him. I like to refer to it as the place of No Can Do. When you survey your present circumstances and future possibilities, God wants you to look away from yourself saying, "I cannot do it." He wants you to settle in the land of No Can Do.

The attitude God desires to permeate and dominate your life is one of surrender. You are to surrender yourself and yield to His control and sufficiency. It is when you recognize the utter futility and folly of trusting in your abilities, capabilities, strengths, experience, spouse, family, friends, finances, education, connections, and whatever else you might be trusting. The Bible says, "I can do all things through Christ Jesus which strengtheneth me" (Philippians 4:13). Paul is teaching us that a total reliance upon God, not our fleshly strength, will give us the sufficiency to meet the expectations, demands, challenges, and trials we encounter. As long as you try to do what needs to be done, you will live in the dishonorable land of I Can Do. Only that which is inspired by God, motivated by love, and done through His Spirit will glorify and exalt Jesus Christ.

Those who prefer to live in the land of I Can Do would rewrite the biblical account of a young warrior named David. He was a young man when he became the king of Israel. Before he was King, he was a shepherd. God used his time in the field to prepare him for greater challenges. One such moment came in the form of a giant man called Goliath. The Philistine soldier evoked fear in the hearts of the Israelite army with his persistent threats. No one would confront the giant until David heard about it. The Old Testament does not give an account of young David trusting a sling and a handful of rocks. Stones or no stones, David surveyed a nine-foot, antagonistic giant and proclaimed, "I come to thee in the name of the Lord of Hosts" (1 Samuel 17:45). Surely, David had used a sling to slay wild beasts. But he lived with a rejection of his personal abilities and a reception of God's! He did not come against Goliath in the name of granite, leather, or his past experience. David approached the battlefield with faith in God. He came depending on God to defeat the enemy, and that is exactly what happened! David did not see the challenge as something he could handle. He saw it as something God could handle!

As long as you deem life as something you can handle, you will continue to live outside the land of No Can Do. God wants us to see life as something only we can handle as we allow Him to handle it on our behalf. If you trust yourself for that which you feel comfortable attempting, and trust God for the rest, you are not in the land of No Can Do. You will continue to see the Goliaths of life run roughshod over you. God wants you to live and abide in the land of No Can Do. Any other approach to life contradicts Jesus' words, "For apart from Me, you can do nothing" (John 15:5).

What is the giant in your life? Perhaps it is the day in and day out rearing of young children. Is it an unreasonable boss? Are you facing financial collapse? Is your giant a sin or habit that you find yourself confessing over and over? Perhaps it is a class you cannot pass. Maybe it is an area of service God is calling you to become involved. Maybe it is an intense trial or a myriad of problems. Is it something trivial or small? Do you have an ungodly attitude, an unforgiving spirit, or the molten lava of bitterness searing the sweetness of your heart? Are there difficult people intricately placed in your life? What heartaches are you facing? What grievous circumstances are you bearing? What load is on your shoulders? What is your Goliath?

God has a wonderful way of leading us into the realm of carnal abandonment. He knows how much aggravation, grief, adversity, and failure it will take to show us our need of Him. He knows how to get us to surrender and yield to His control. God uses these intersections of life to collide our self-reliance with the reality of our insufficiency. Because God only receives glory for that which He does, it is a privilege for Him to challenge us beyond the abilities of our fleshly capabilities! He wants you in the land of No Can Do.

I want to show you how to live in such a manner as to bring God optimal glory, even through the excruciating and difficult times of life. The Old Testament records the story of a woman thrust into the land of No Can Do. Second Kings 4:1–7 portrays the dilemma of a widow left with a load of financial debt she was unable to pay.

"Now there cried a certain woman of the wives of the sons of the prophets unto Elisha saying, 'Thy servant my husband is dead; and thou knowest that thy servant did fear the LORD: and the creditor is come to take unto him my two sons to be bondmen.' And Elisha said unto her, 'What shall I do for thee? Tell me, what hast thou in the House?' And she said, 'Thine handmaid hath not any thing in the house, save a pot of oil.' Then he said, 'Go, borrow thee vessels abroad of all thy neighbours, even empty vessels; borrow not a few. And when thou art come in, thou shalt shut the door upon thee and thy sons, and shalt pour into all those vessels, and thou shalt set aside that which is full.' So she went from him, and shut the door upon her and upon her sons, who brought the vessels to her; and she poured out. And it came to pass, when the vessels were full, that she said unto her son, 'Bring me yet a vessel.' And he said unto her, 'There is not a vessel more.' And the oil stayed. Then she came and told the man of God, and he said, 'Go, sell the oil, and pay thy debt, and live thou and thy children of the rest.' "

The narrative is a wonderful illustration of how God wants us to thrive in our troubles. More than once have I heard Dr. Adrian Rogers say, "God did not come to get us out of trouble but to get into it with us." Second Kings revealed a woman in trouble. Her husband's untimely death left her in financial shambles, and she was facing the reality of paying her debt with the fellowship and freedom of her two sons. However, as Daniel found God with him in his fiery trial, the widow was about to find God in the midst of her giant problem. She had a giant challenge!

First, note *she had in indebtedness because someone related to her died.* Verse 1 says, "My husband is dead and the creditors have come." I am reminded every time I read this verse of the indebtedness that I have to live for God because someone related to me died. I am a child of God because Jesus Christ died on Calvary's cross. I live with an acute desire to please God with my life. We could never pay Him back for His salvation or the many blessings He lavishes upon us. However, if it were possible, we should desire to repay Him infinite degrees! I have a deep sense of gratitude in my heart for God's gift of faith and work of grace in my heart. I am deeply and forever indebted to God because of the death of Jesus my Lord. I want to be loving, joyful, peaceful, gentle, forgiving, faithful, and patient. I desire to be a bold witness for the Son of God. I want to be the fragrance of Christ to a lost and dying world. I want to honor God through the difficult times of life.

If you do not have the desire to honor God with your life, then you have good reason to question the reality of your salvation. When I ponder the cross in my heart, an undeniable and inescapable desire wells up within my soul to glorify the King of kings. As a child of God, I am forever indebted to the Son of God. The widow had a debt because someone related to her died, and so do I. His name is Jesus.

Secondly, *she did not have it in and of herself to pay back the debt.* She could not do it. In verse 2, the prophet questions her available resources. She says, "Thine handmaid hath nothing in the house, save a pot of oil." Of course, a jar of oil was not sufficient to pay a debt commensurate with the taking of her sons. The woman did not have the ability to pay the debt. I am reminded by this verse of my inability to fulfill my indebtedness to live for God. I do not have the resources in my flesh to honor and glorify God. I do not have the ability to live for Jesus apart from the enabling work of God's grace in my heart. The Bible says, "For I know that in me (that is, in my flesh,) dwelleth no good thing" (Romans 7:18). God demands holiness in my relationship with Him, but my flesh cannot produce holiness. We need to stop trying to get our flesh to act right. We need to stop trying to get our carnality to behave properly. If you trust your flesh to respond properly to the storms of life, you will be found lacking every time. God's goodness and grace demands that we honor Him through the disappointments and disasters of life. Apart from the Holy Spirit, I do not possess the ability to shine faithfully and consistently for Him through every task and trial. I have nothing in the house except a jar of oil. Humanly speaking, this widow did not have the ability to fulfill the obligation—nor do you.

Thank God the story does not end there. She learns a pivotal truth regarding the benevolence of our Lord. The prophet asks, "What shall I do for thee?" The man of God is representative of God Himself. *The woman learns she has the willingness of God to get involved.* She begins to understand God's desire to demonstrate His power through her dilemma.

God asks the same question of us today. He asks you right this very moment, "What do you need Me to do for you?" Ponder the thought. Would it have been wise and acceptable if the widow had exclaimed, "I need you to do everything. Meet this demand in my life today. I cannot do it." This is the response of those living in the land of No Can Do. There is a song that talks about our inability to walk without God holding our hands. Friend, my heart cannot beat nor my lungs expand without the working of God. I cannot get up to walk without Him. I do not want Him to hold my hand. I need Him to hold me completely. We are totally dependent upon Him. Isn't it amazing that we are so totally dependent on Him, yet we are not depending totally on Him?

Have you ever heard someone teach or quote 1 Corinthians 10:13 out of context? The text deals with temptation but many have applied it to adversity saying, "God will not put more on you than you can bear." What does one mean by that? I have experienced some difficulties I know were too much for me to bear. I have witnessed others who encountered trials that make mine look elementary. God does put more on us than we can bear. God has put more on us than we can bear. The demands of Scripture are more than I can meet. I am not able to live the Word in my own strength. The Lord Jesus says, "Apart from Me, you can do nothing" (John 15:5, New American Standard). When I was a pastor, we had an evangelist preach a series of meetings on spiritual renewal. I remember Dr. Ron Lynch saying, "I am nothing. That's a zero with the rim knocked off." Dr. Lynch continued, "I used to fear being a failure until I realized I am one." God will put more on us than we can handle, but He will never put more on us than He can handle. He can handle anything!

Oh, how God wants to knock the props out from under us that are robbing Him of His glory and rightful place to meet our needs. Psalm 20:7 says, "Some trust in chariots, and some in horses: but we will remember the name of the Lord our God." Are you tired of trying to be nice to those who are not kind to you? Are you tired of wearing that fleshly mask of joy? Are you ready to shed your life of the façades? I do not want to flounder around in life as I attempt to live for God through my flesh. Have you ever noticed how ugly a flounder is? They are unattractive fish. Many in the church are floundering in their Christian experience and making ugly messes of their lives. They do not know God still asks, "What shall I do for thee?" Yes, the widow had the willingness of God to get involved.

Have you ever thought of the way we ask God to get involved? We pray like this, "Lord, help me to be patient today." Or, we pray, "God, I need You to help me be loving toward so-and-so today." God does not want to help us. Sometimes I think we ask in this manner with this pattern of thinking: "Lord, as I try to please You with my flesh today, pick up the slack and make up for difference as I fall short." Asking for help can imply your involvement. When a person is drowning, a wise person will wait for that individual to give up before attempting a rescue lest the victim pull them both under!

I do not want to get on a semantic merry-go-round, but it is important that you investigate your approach to the Christian life. Is your plea for help an indication of your dual dependence on God and yourself? Yes, the Holy Spirit is our resident Helper. The implication is not His helping me as I live but as I die to my efforts. Who needs the most help? People who are dead, or people who are alive? I choose to die daily and moment- by-moment.

The widow learned another profound truth. *She possessed an unrealized and untapped resource.* As a matter of fact, she is about to realize her only source of power and sufficiency. Second Kings 4:2 says, "Thine handmaid hath not any thing in the house, save a pot of oil." Often, oil is symbolic in the Bible of the Holy Spirit. Notice the oil in her pantry becomes the solution to her trial. She had an untapped and unrealized resource. I am mindful of Zechariah 4:6, "Not by might, nor by power, but by my Spirit, saith the Lord of hosts." The widow has only one jar of oil. She had only one resource. She had a jar of oil. When you placed your personal faith in Jesus Christ alone for salvation, He deposited the oil of the Holy Spirit into the pantry of your heart! Ephesians 1:13–14 says, "In whom ye also trusted, after that ye heard the word of truth, the gospel of your salvation: in whom also after that ye believed, ye were sealed with that Holy Spirit of promise. Which is the earnest of our inheritance until the redemption of the purchased possession, unto the praise of His glory." Romans 8:9 states, "Now if any man have not the Spirit of Christ, he is none of His." He is your resident resource. Just as that jar of oil became the solution in the widow's dilemma, so too is He the solution to the challenges you encounter. He is the solution to your lack of love and joy. He is the solution to your need of peace and patience. He is the unrealized and untapped source of kindness and faithfulness you so desire to exude. He is your victory over every bad habit. He is your source of strength in the midst of trial and heartache.

As an evangelist, I have enjoyed the privilege of traveling to many churches to share the Word. I love people, and I love the church. Jesus died for the church. The church is the pillar of truth in the world. I have a deep concern, however, for the health of His church. Jesus taught the gates of hell will not prevail against us, but they are impacting and influencing us. They are not prevailing but they are assailing! In too many realms, the church is pathetic because she is so apathetic. Why is the church so spiritually apathetic? I believe we have been defeated and discouraged for so long we have become disillusioned watching the failures of the flesh. We have been impotent and spiritually anemic for so long that we have become apathetic. We are so anemic because we have looked to ourselves rather than the One who made us! We have trusted our power rather than His. We are so atrophic because we are malnourished. We need the nutrition and vitality only God the Holy Spirit gives. God wants His church to repent, and He will use the power of His Word or the persuasion of adversity to show us our need. It is not by our might or power. It is by His Spirit. God does not say, "It is by your might plus My Spirit." Our resource is the Holy Spirit plus nothing. The resource is the source. The time is now for you to realize Who is in your heart and tap into His anointing and empowerment.

The widow was on the road to discovering her needs will never be larger than God's ability! I believe I know what you may be thinking, "But you do not understand what I am going through." You may be saying, "God has allowed me to go through some trials that are just too much to bear." I want you to reread verse 3. The Bible says, "Then he said, 'Go, borrow thee vessels abroad of all thy neighbors, even empty vessels; borrow not a few.'" Do you perceive a challenge? The man of God is thinking, "God likes a challenge. Get as many as you can find. You are about to see that a challenge to a sovereign, almighty God is no challenge at all. You will never bring more vessels than He can fill."

Friend, may I say that God will never allow you to have a need greater than His ability and willingness to fulfill it! My greatest problems and challenges will never exhaust His sufficiency. My most dire straits will never exceed His supply of grace. Although my experience might be dredging the dark, muddy depths of the worst life has to offer, it will never get so dark that God's grace is not sufficient. No matter how dark the night might become, He can always put stars in the sky! When the waters of life get clouded with care, He will give me a mask, provide me a light, settle the silt, clear the water, or bring me up! Either way, I will be supplied with the sufficiency of the Holy Spirit! He is the Good Shepherd. When the pasture of my life becomes brown, barren, and overgrazed, He will lead me to green pastures. If the droughts of life scorch the blissful glow of my countenance, He will supply joy. He is not merely a mighty God; He is the Almighty God!

Elisha tells the widow, "Don't get a few." He wanted the circumstances arranged in such a manner that she would know subsequently that God alone met the need. Have you ever gone through a trial and looking back, you knew God got you through it? When I get to heaven, I would like to be able to reflect upon the memories of my life and point to every aspect of them and say, "Lord Jesus, You deserve the credit for how I did that. I yielded and surrendered. You did the rest." If God deems it right to fill my life with a multitude of adverse and difficult vessels, then I will have the privilege and joy of watching Him supernaturally fill them with provisions of divine grace! Note in verse 6 how the flow of God's provision ceases. When the need is met, His provision ends—ready to meet the next challenge! If you have a blue-colored need, God will provide blue-colored grace. No matter the need, God will match it.

How does one experience the provision of God's grace? You must simply abide in Him by trusting in His sufficiency and yielding for His provision. When God chooses to portray us as in it for nothing, how should we live as to remain faithful to the call? Elisha commands the widow in verse 4 saying, "And when thou art come in, thou shalt shut the door upon thee and upon thy sons, and shalt pour out into all those vessels, and thou shalt set aside that which is full." *She learned the need of going behind closed doors with God.* You will never see the divine, dynamic provision of God until you make your daily time with God the priority of your life. I do not retreat daily with God to have a "quiet time." I go behind closed doors to have a "loud time." When you really have a quiet time with the Lord, inevitably, it will be a loud time. He will speak loudly and clearly. It is God speaking to me and me speaking to Him! It is noisy when God fills this empty vessel with the water of His Spirit!

The sinful displays of the flesh are God's way of alerting me of my neglect. It is during those times that God reminds me my closed-door fellowship with Him is lacking. When I am aggravated, impatient, short-fused, unkind, unloving, and lacking joy, I know my heart is not yielded to the Holy Spirit. I am amazed how God allows just enough ungodly people into my life at just the right times in order to get my attention. When I neglect personal time with God, I declare my ignorance by taking the reins of my life, thus proclaiming confidence in myself rather than Almighty God. When I neglect to walk with God moment-by-moment with a keen awareness of Him, I am in danger of seeing the fruit of my feeble flesh. We must make our daily devotion with God as much a top priority as our continuous fellowship. He wants you to walk continuously with Him. He wants you to walk constantly and consistently with Him. He wants you to walk in cadence with Him. Your life with God is not a success just because you have a daily quiet time. But that is the place to start.

The point of this chapter is to help you get to the wonderful point of saying, "Alright, Lord, life is too much for me to handle. Your standard for my life is too great for me to reach in my strength. I cannot live the Christian life." If you are arriving there, you are on your way to an incredible journey with Jesus! Are you living in the land of No Can Do? Are you tired of seeing the fruit of your efforts? Are you ready to see the power of God in your life? Are you ready to experience victory? Obey the Word of God, and be filled with the Holy Spirit! Get into the glorious land of No Can Do. Stay there! Live there. Abide there.

Chapter 9

SPIRITUAL WARFARE: OUR BATTLE ENEMY

"Be strong in the Lord . . ." (Ephesians 6:10)

Warren Wiersbe expressed it best, "Sooner or later every believer discovers that the Christian life is a battleground, not a playground, and that he faces an enemy who is much stronger than he is—apart from the Lord."[1] The Christian life is not a grocery store where we pick and choose the items we desire off the shelves of God's will. Neither is it is not an amusement park. The Christian life is a battleground. Sometimes the battle gets intense and the church has little intuition in light of the opportunity to honor or dishonor God. Spiritual warfare is not an option but is necessary for optimal precision in waging the war that brings honor to the King of kings. If you ignore this vital element in your Christian experience, you will never know the victorious Christian experience. Spiritual warfare is not just about getting the devil out of your life, but honoring God when He allows Satan to come into it.

The book of Ephesians is organized in a very telling manner. The arrangement of the contents gives insight into the vulnerable areas of our lives and the value of emphasizing crucial aspects of Christian practice. Chapter 5 teaches us about Spirit-filled living. Chapter 6 instructs us concerning spiritual warfare. Sandwiched between these topics are the most common relationships of life. These chapters give us wisdom regarding church life (5:21), married life (verses 22–33), home life (6:1–4), and work life (verses 5–9). All of these involve people interacting with one another. Where there are two people, there exists the possibility for strife. They are the vulnerable and volatile areas of our lives where the devil often aims his wicked arrows. The Bible says, "Where no oxen are, the crib is clean" (Proverbs 14:4). Oftentimes, the adversity we encounter has its beginning in one of these realms, and people are usually involved. I find it interesting that God's Spirit leads Paul to sandwich these relationships between the mandates of Spirit-filled living and spiritual warfare. It is not enough to live the Spirit-filled life. God is teaching us the necessity and value of waging a spiritual war.

The armor God supplies is sufficient for us to encounter the most vicious and heavy artillery of the enemy. God warns us not to be partially clad in verse 11 saying, "Put on the whole armor." We are to put on the entire supply of God's defensive and offensive mechanisms. The choice is simple—don the armor or get done in by the adversary. A partially clad warrior will become a pitifully sad warrior. A fully clad warrior will be a fully glad warrior. When you realize the ferocity and tenacity of the enemy, you will understand the need for the whole armor.

The United States Air Force has spent billions of dollars building bombers that are able to go into the enemy's domain nearly undetected by radar. Stealth bombers are so effective because the enemy does not know they are there until it is too late.

I have seen the devil do so much damage over the years. There are many men I personally knew in the ministry who have been taken out by the enemy. We do not have to live unaware of the enemy and his approach. The radar of God's Word has forever removed Satan's stealthy capabilities. We can detect him before he gets in view. I agree with Judson Cornwall's words, "We will not be set free by knowing our enemy; we will be set free by knowing our deliverer, the Lord Jesus Christ!"[2] However, one should not underestimate the need for understanding the basics of who Satan is and how he functions.

God's Word reveals our battle enemy: "Finally, my brethren, be strong in the Lord, and in the power of His might. Put on the whole armour of God, that ye may be able to stand against the wiles of the devil. For we wrestle not against flesh and blood, but against powers, against the rulers of the darkness of this world, against spiritual wickedness in high places" (Ephesians 6:10–12).

We have a **strong** enemy in this battle. Why would God command us to embrace His strength as opposed to our own? Because we cannot fight a supernatural battle with natural strength! We have a supernatural, strong enemy. We would be foolish to encounter him in our strength. Just ask Samson! He died a disgraceful death with his eyes gouged out because somewhere along the way he forgot his strength was actually God's. You are no match for your enemy. You need the power of God.

Our adversary is strong, and he is also a **sly** enemy. We have a wily enemy who is always looking for a way to take us out of the race and get us on the sidelines. We are to put on the armor of God that we may stand against the wiles of the devil. When I was growing up, it was common for many children to spend their Saturday mornings watching a series of cartoons called

"The Bugs Bunny/Road Runner Hour." One episode involved a coyote that was always trying to enter a fold of sheep and steal a meal. The sheepdog always thwarted the coyote's plans, but that wily coyote kept conjuring up ways to try again.

As God's children, we have an enemy who is looking for ways to take us down. Right now, he has a plan. If that plan fails, he will have another. He wants to mar the sanctification God is working in you. He wants to use you to discredit the reality of God's presence in your life in the minds of those who watch you. He wants to implement a scheme of spiritual demolition that the little boats, prisoners, and jailors in your life will doubt the validity of your claim to know Him. He wants them to reject the notion of God's reality or the relationship you have with Him. The devil has a plan. He is a slick, sly schemer.

We have a **satanic** enemy. Verse 11 compels us to stand against the schemes of the devil. The enemy is called by two names, each revealing his purpose and method in the fight. He is the devil, our accuser. He is Satan, our adversary. He fulfills his purpose and employs his methods through strategies of deception. As our accuser, Satan seeks to tear us down mentally and wear us down morally. He wants you to lose morale as a committed, sold-out, loyal, obedient soldier. He will accuse you of impure motives. He will accuse you of being unacceptable to God. He will accuse you of being lost, deceived and ignorant. He will lie to you. As your adversary, the devil will oppose you through temptation, adversity, and strife. He will work often against you through people. Satan will come against you through circumstances. Your enemy is satanic.

Closely related to this is the next revelation of our enemy in verse 12: "We wrestle not against flesh and blood." We have a **spiritual** enemy. Flesh and blood represents humanity. Satan will not remind you that your enemy is not people. He wants you to forget that you have a spiritual enemy. He will not remind you that your contention with people is not rooted in people. He wants you to think people are the problem. He wants you to believe you are merely battling church people, in-laws, family, neighbors, co-workers, or your spouse.

How is it possible to live with people and love people despite the mischief they incite, the mishandlings they perform, and misadventures they inspire? Our Lord Jesus reveals a more formidable enemy than often occurs to us. When He was informing the disciples of His impending betrayal and death at Calvary, Simon Peter opposed the thought saying, "Be it far from Thee, Lord: this shall never be" (Matthew 16:22). Peter was disapproving of and discouraging our Savior's procurement of our eternal destiny afforded only through the cross. Jesus' response is a very clear and telling reminder of our real enemy. Cognizant He was not battling mere flesh and blood, Jesus says, "Get thee behind me, Satan" (verse 23). Jesus had the spiritual perception to know His opposition ultimately was not Peter. He perceived a spiritual enemy—Satan.

When people are unreasonable and problematic, you will do well to respond with the same spiritual perception. Many trials in life can be traced back to a satanic source. He is always attempting to tempt us. Satan wants to enrage, exploit, and exaggerate the words people use and utter. Yes, people will be held accountable for how they allowed the devil to use them, but the bottom line is Satan. Jesus saw the activity of Satan behind the words of Peter. As a puppeteer brings animation by the slipping of a hand into a puppet, so too the devil slips his vile hand into the lives of people, even Christian people, to animate them for a script written in hell.

How can one live above the unjust actions of others and resist the possibility of bitter feelings? It is possible to love people who are responsible for the adversity that unfairly touches your life. Jesus exemplified His love for Satan's puppets when on the cross He cried, "Father, forgive them, they know not what they do" (Luke 23:34). Uttering these immortal words, Jesus revealed His awareness that Golgotha had become the stage for a puppet show of satanic proportions. If you fail to see the difficulties and heartaches of life involving people as satanic, you will become cold, bitter, distant, and ineffective for the kingdom of God. Bitterness is a grudge you can nurse, but it will never get better. If you have anger leading to an unforgiving spirit, the devil will pitch his tent in the campground of your heart, and he will light the campfire of bitterness until it consumes the sweet, soft marshmallows of your fellowship with God and man. The smoke will spread to those camping near your life, ruining their desire to be with you or to follow your witness.

Jesus was kind and forgiving of those who *unjustly* mocked Him. Only the Spirit-filled can respond in such a manner. Only those with the spiritual perception of the Lord Jesus to know the enemy is spiritual may remain Spirit-filled through the adversities of life.

Also, we have a **stubborn** enemy. The Bible says, "For we wrestle . . ." (verse 12). The verb is a present tense verb, indicative of continuous activity. Your battle is ongoing. Your strong, sly enemy is relentlessly and tenaciously warring against God through you. The devil is utterly convinced he can thwart God's plan for your life. Have you ever wondered why difficulties seem to come so frequently at times? Will the devil ever give up on me and move on to others? Will life ever become carefree? Not until we get to Heaven. The Scriptures reveal our enemy as a stubborn foe. Through his demons, he will keep coming back and back and back and back and back. "Our struggle is" implies our battle as an ongoing affair. The battle is called a struggle. If you seem to be in a lull, the enemy has merely gone underground. He will be back. As much as God never sleeps nor slumbers, this verse implies the same of our enemy. Just as Jesus is a seeker of men, so too is the devil—for different reasons, of course! You might think about skipping a semester or a class at the University of Adversity, but the devil intends for you to be in class all the time! You might relax, but the devil never does. Like the cat you once fed on the doorstep of your home, the devil will keep returning again and again. We never have the luxury of letting down our guard.

Chapter 10

SPIRITUAL WARFARE: OUR BATTLE EQUIPMENT

"That you might be able to stand . . ." (Ephesians 6:11)

The armor God supplies is essential for maintaining a consistent response toward the difficult moments of life. His armor is necessary for a godly response toward God and man. Much of Satan's activity is intricately connected with difficult circumstances. Some of these are small, aggravating situations, and others are profoundly difficult and sad. The armor God supplies is sufficient for any attack the devil might wage against us! Whether one is facing personal temptations to sin or personal trials that spoil one's joy or peace, His provision is sufficient. The armor is necessary for enduring and succeeding in every aspect of the Christian life—temptations, tests, or trials. I will focus on the relationship of the armor and the trials we encounter.

How does spiritual warfare aid one in daily living when trials and difficulties come? The daily donning of God's armor is necessary to glorify Him consistently. The Bible describes it in

Ephesians 6:14–17: "Stand therefore, having your loins girt about with truth, and having on the breastplate of righteousness; And your feet shod with the preparation of the gospel of peace; Above all, taking the shield of faith, wherewith ye shall be able to quench all the fiery darts of the wicked. And take the helmet of salvation, and the sword of the Spirit, which is the Word of God."

One of the most common mistakes we make in the Christian life is to forget a battle is always being waged against us. We never have the luxury of getting out of bed in the morning and neglecting to prepare ourselves spiritually to meet the day. With the dawning of a new day comes the dawning of renewed advances of our formidable foe. He is intent on disrupting, dissuading, disarming, dismantling and discouraging our walk with God. The goal of our enemy is to dilute our convictions or to dissolve our consecration. He wants to disintegrate your affection for God and man. The devil seeks to disrupt your fellowship with God and man.

When upheaval invades your life, or the little aggravations of life begin to nip at your spirit, the armor of God is made available for your consistent response and continued resolve to honor God. You can have a good day on a bad day. Your spiritual skin can remain dry, though the disheartening raindrops of enemy attack pelt relentlessly against your. The Holy Spirit supplies the perfect protection of His spiritual armor enabling us to prevail against the elements that assail. Despite how you might feel from time to time, He has never, and will never, leave you out in the cold without providing the coat and gloves of His spiritual armor! Let's look at the components.

Truth

The Bible teaches in Ephesians 6:13 that we are to "gird our loins with truth." Understand that the apostle Paul was in a Roman prison as he wrote these words. I can imagine him bound hand and foot, fastened to a wall in a prison guarded tenaciously by a Roman soldier. As his eyes scanned the armor of his guardian adversary, Paul became riveted on the idea of the guard's long, flowing robe retrieved, tucked, and fastened securely by a belt around the guard's waist. Paul noted how the guard was ready to respond to any revolt or challenge from the prisoners. His robe would not get in the way of his offense and defense.

Suddenly, imagine the Holy Spirit speaks to Paul saying, "His belt should remind you of the truth you are to submit to and abide in as you endure this trial. It is a life submitted to living within and remaining in the truth, the confines and boundaries of the whole of My Word. You are to have the mindset and heart that desires and devotes itself to living within the realm of My Word, whatever it asks or however it leads. This is the way you will preclude any spiritual tripping during this trial. Make up your mind to submit and yield to My lordship every moment of every day."

When the Lord allows demonic forces to give you fits, you remain fit with a life submitted and committed to remaining true to the entire revelation of the Word of God. No attitude, action, response, and feeling will be allowed to venture beyond the boundaries of the Bible. You must get up and live every day with the pursuit of God, desirous to master the truth and to be mastered by it. It is a daily decision to live with the loins of your life hemmed in and secured by the Word of God, regardless of what it says. I am talking about a heart that is desirous to live within the generic and general confines and haven of the Bible.

The belt of truth is a life desirous, determined, and dedicated to living within the parameters of God's truth, the Word and will of God. My desire to live within these parameters defines how much I care about holiness and righteous living.

If you do not have a desire to gird your loins with truth, you will never thrive in the land of No Can Do. You will do well to survive. Never forget this: merely surviving does not bring God glory. Thriving brings glory and honor to the King. Think of ways the devil lies to you when you go through difficulties. He often says something like this, "God must not be happy with you. He must not be on your side right now. What have you done to cause Him to rise up against you? He must have something against you." Oh, how the forces of hell attempt to rob us of our peace by causing us to question our standing with God. Satan wants us to live in fear. He attempts to erode our peace by evoking questions of whether we have stepped outside God's protective and loving arms. The devil would have you believe God is angry with you. He wants to inflict your soul with ill feelings toward God. He wants you to begin holding a grudge toward the Lord.

Nothing gives me more peace and confidence in life than knowing my heart is submitted to the Lordship of Jesus. I'm not speaking necessarily of a submission to the specific commands of His Word, but to a blanket embracing of His Word, the truth. Knowing my heart is yielded to whatever He commands and desires for my life gives me confidence, regardless of what He allows me to go through, because I know my circumstances are not a result of my having ventured outside the protective haven of His will. I know that He is on my side. As a child of God, I know He is always on my side, but it is another thing to experience Him as on our side. The Bible teaches, "God is love" (1 John 4:16). But God says, "I love those who love me"

(Proverbs 8:17). God loves everyone, but only those committed and submitted to Him will experience what He is. When I go through harrowing times, I may doubt and ponder many things, but I do not have to wonder if God is for me when my heart is girded with truth. When my life across the board is yielded to Jesus as Lord, I have confidence through faith that I am abiding in His loving care and concern. As we shall see, this powerful knowledge touches and impacts every other part of God's armor.

Righteousness

The breastplate of righteousness is necessary for protecting your heart against the lies of the devil when he attempts to depress and discourage your heart and mind. I cannot stress the importance of getting up every day and donning the righteousness of God. You must get up and live every moment, reminding yourself of the imputed and imparted righteousness of Jesus Christ. Righteousness is to be right with God. It has a positional and practical application. As to my position in Christ, I am eternally righteous in God's sight and right with Him forever. Philippians 3:9 states, "And found in Him, not having mine own righteousness, which is of the law, but that which is through the faith of Christ, the righteousness which is of God by faith."

When I received Jesus Christ as my personal Lord and Savior, God began to view me and accept me as righteous. Although I still sin at times, God sees me as He sees His Son through the imputed righteousness of Jesus Christ. I am clean by the blood of Jesus. I am a child of God. The righteousness of Jesus has been imputed to my once bankrupt, spiritual account. This is my righteous position in Christ! Because of this, I know God is on my side!

Practically, I have walked with the Lord long enough to know my experience does not always match my position in Christ. There are times I sin against the Lord and live unrighteously. During these times, my practice does not match and mesh with my position. I am to get up and live every day walking the fence-line of my heart, inspecting it for breaches, holes and breaks caused by sin. I am to look for places where I am not right with God. These holes in the armor leave us vulnerable to the attacks of Satan. During difficult times, you will be tempted with ungodly thoughts. You will detect the enemy leading you down the road of bitter persuasion and wrong thinking. When you were saved by God's grace, the Lord built the fence of righteousness around your heart. You must get up every day and remind yourself whose you are and whom you are. You are God's, and you are to be godly.

Reminding yourself daily of the positional helps you to continue dying to yourself, your rights, and your desires. This is important when going through difficulties to keep the right tenderness and sweetness of heart. The devil will say you deserve better; positional righteousness will remind you that you are bought with a price. The devil will lead you into wrong patterns of thinking, but practicing righteousness will preclude the enemy from injecting his venomous lies into our minds and hearts. The position serves to remind you of who you are. Practical righteousness helps you remain experientially what you are with regard to positional righteousness. A daily donning of the breastplate of imputed righteousness serves as a reminder of who the boss is. This promotes accountability with your Lord. A daily donning of the breastplate of imparted righteousness serves to seal any openings for the fiery darts of enemy temptation to sit, sulk, and soar in spirit.

Peace

Ephesians 6:15 teaches us to shod our feet "with the preparation of the gospel of peace." What does this mean, and what does it have to do with trials? How does one have peace with God except through a reception of the gospel of Jesus Christ? His death on Calvary's cross is the way of peace with God. Having received peace with God affords us the glorious peace *of* God through the trials and uncertainties of this life. As a child of God, my heart is prepared for the battles of this life because I have received the gospel of Jesus Christ.

Any military soldier must have a certain amount of security that leads to confidence in the field of battle. This confidence leads to an intrinsic peace of mind. One is enabled to keep a level head. He has a good head on his shoulders. The feet of Ephesians 6:15 discusses the sure footing of the soldier in battle. Spikes driven through the soles of a Roman soldier's shoes provided extra security in the heat of battle. The spikes provided a more sure footing. Would you rather go through hand-to-hand combat with your feet slipping or with solid, sure footing?

I have seen a lot of people walking at a guilty distance from the Lord Jesus because they began to slip and slide during a difficult time of uncertainty. Do you know why Christians seem to be walking with God on an ice skating rink? They do not have their feet prepared. Ephesians 6:15 tells us to have our feet prepared. Remember, since you have received Jesus as Lord and Savior, you have the sandals in hand (heart), but do you have them on your feet?

Here's the crucial thing to understand about your battle shoes. Without your feet prepared with the gospel of peace, you will not have peace. Peace comes from having become a child of

God. Because I have received Jesus Christ, all of God's promises are mine. The promises of God provide the spikes in our spirits that keep our mental and spiritual footing sure and secure in the heat of battle. From whence does our peace come? From resting in the promises of God that are ours because we are His! A lack of trust in God's promises will leave you lacking peace of mind and heart in the trials and throes of life. You will find yourself fearful, irritable, aggravated, weakened, confused, vulnerable, and insecure.

When you read the whole of God's Word, there are *three general promises* revealed to every child of God. They are indispensable for our spiritual health and vigor, especially during times of uncertainty, grief, sadness, and pain. It is imperative that you begin donning this armor on a daily basis before trouble comes, for you do not know when it will come your way.

The first promise is eternal life. Jesus says, "And I give them eternal life, and they shall never perish, neither shall any man pluck them out of my hand" (John 10:28). God's promise of eternal life lets me know that the worst thing that might ever happen to me (to be killed) will be the best thing that ever happened to me. Lord willing, I will get on a plane next week and travel 5500 miles to Argentina to preach the gospel. When the devil begins to wage a battle of intimidation in my heart about the jet crashing in the mountains of Brazil, my heart and mind are guarded with great peace knowing God has promised me everlasting life. The great promise of eternal life is mine because I have prepared my feet through a reception of the gospel of peace!

The worst thing that can happen to a child of God is actually the best. Death is the doorway that leads to eternal life. As God's children, death is a true friend. God would never want you to read these words and use them as an excuse to commit suicide in order to escape your problems. You do not have the right to determine the length of your earthly existence. That is God's prerogative. When a Christian commits suicide, they tell the world that Jesus is not sufficient to meet the demands and challenges we face. Suicide is a bad mistake and cop out.

Perhaps you are facing a potentially life-threatening situation. Maybe you have received an ominous report from your doctor. When our daughter died, I found great peace and strength in knowing we will meet again. Perhaps you have lost a loved one, and you do not have assurance they had a personal relationship with Jesus Christ. You can have peace knowing that heaven will still be heaven, even if you get there and discover they are absent. Heaven will be heaven because Jesus is there, not because your loved ones are there. Jesus declares, "And if I go and prepare a place for you, I will come again, and receive you to Myself; *that where I am,* there you may be also" (John 14:3, New American Standard). Yes, Jesus has a sure future for us. Thank God for the promise of eternal life!

The second general promise for every child of God is the promise of a guided life. Sometimes we go through real times of uncertainty. It occurs through the loss of a job or the marital unfaithfulness of a spouse. Sometimes uncertainty comes through mere demonic panic attacks rooted in no real or tangible circumstance. There is just a foreboding sense of insecurity and uncertainty. Peace for the battle is ours because of the promise of God to provide us a guided life. The Bible says, "Trust in the Lord with all of your heart, and lean not on your own understanding. In all your ways acknowledge Him, and He will make your path straight" (Proverbs 3:5–6). A straight path means that He will lead you down the road He has planned for you. Jesus Christ is the Good Shepherd (John 10). A good shepherd will not lead his sheep into a pasture not good for his flock. Every field He leads us is the best for grazing! God will see to it that His sheep are feeding on the most green, lush, chlorophyll-laden fields available. "The Lord is My Shepherd, *I shall not want*" (Psalm 23:1).

The promise of a guided life affords us peace, as we trust Him as the Good Shepherd. He is leading you in the straight path. Be careful to understand that the straight path is not the path that makes the most sense. Just ask the Hebrews in the Old Testament as God led them out of Egypt by way of the Red Sea. The way of the Red Sea was not the most direct geographical route to the Promised Land, but it was the straight way because it was God's plan and will. What did not make sense to them made perfect sense to their Shepherd. He knew the path was best. It was straight. And rest assured knowing, if He leads you in, He will lead you out! If God brings you to it, then He will bring you through it!

Are you trusting God to be faithful as your Good Shepherd? He does not fill the position on a part-time basis. Always and forever, He is the Good Shepherd. I have confidence and courage to face today and tomorrow because the One who has planned my life is the One who is leading my life.

The third promise is for a victorious life. If I dare meet the day without these spikes in my footwear, I will be apt to slip here and there nearly every day. The Bible says, "And we know that God is working all things together for good to those who love God and are called according to His promise" (Romans 8:28). He promises a victorious life! The victory lies in the fact that regardless of what might touch my life, whether big or small, just or unjust, fair or unfair, all of them will work for my good! Perhaps you have made some mistakes in life, and the devil has lied to you saying, "Your life will never be right, now." Maybe you have lost your job and you have heard Satan whisper, "You are past your prime. The best opportunities are behind you. You will never have another opportunity like you had." Can you imagine a couple past the age of childbearing losing their children in a tragic accident? I can only imagine how the devil would work on their minds, telling them the best of life is behind them. Can you hear Satan speaking lies to a woman whose dream husband has chosen to sin against God and chase another woman? What personal dilemma can you insert into these pages? We all have our stories of disappointment, heartache, and brokenness.

If you have received Jesus as Lord and Savior, you can experience the peace of God despite your experience. No matter how destitute the situation or how impossible it might appear, God is working all of it for my good. It is the confidence we have because it is the promise of God. I remember the testimony of Corrie ten Boom when imprisoned by the Nazis in a World War II concentration camp. She recalled the rancid, filthy surroundings as she awaited her possible execution. Her sister encouraged her to thank God for the flea infestation that made their existence nearly unbearable. Corrie found it hard to thank God for the flea infestation until she learned it was those tiny fleas which discouraged the guards from choosing to enter their barrack. Yes, all things work together, even the tiny things of life. All things are being worked together by God for our good (and His glory). You might feel like a victim right now, but God is going to turn the table! You will see that you are the victor! Thank God for the victory! It is the promise of God.

Faith

When I was about 10, I was tossing the football with some neighborhood pals when one of the guys threw the ball a little short of where I was standing. Not really sure where the ball was going to go, I reached out for it just before it plowed into my nose. Footballs are so hard to predict. They can bounce in unpredictable directions. Footballs remind me of feelings. They are unpredictable, and you can hardly depend on them. Too often Christians live by their feelings rather than faith. "Faith is the assurance of things hoped for and the evidence of things not seen" (Hebrews 11:1). "And without faith it is impossible to please God, for he who comes to God must believe He is, and that He rewards those who diligently seek Him" (Hebrews 11:6). Faith is another part of our armor.

Have you ever gone through a time of potential discouragement? Most of us can pinpoint a time in our lives when we felt disheartened because things were not going according to script—usually our script. The Bible says, "Taking up the shield of faith with which you will be able to extinguish all the flaming missiles of the evil one" (Ephesians 6:16). The missiles of the enemy are usually the thoughts and feelings Satan brings to your mind to get you to disbelieve or doubt what God has said in His Word. Having dressed oneself for spiritual battle with the three basic promises of God, those keys must be hung on the key ring of faith. The devil does not mind if you "shod your feet with the preparation of the gospel of peace" as long as you don't trust God in faith for it. Faith is the way of appropriating all God has for us. Regarding adversity, faith fends off attacks of doubt, unbelief, discouragement, anger, and depression. Faith is taking God at His Word; trusting Him to do it, accomplish it, and be it!

I might seem a little strange to some people, but I believe God is real. I really believe Jesus is alive. Certainly, I believe God is actively controlling my life. He is real. A faith in God that believes He saves the soul from sin must trust the same God to take care of the lesser part—the affairs of our lives. God is real and really is in control. God deeply cares for you. He loves you.

I do not think most who have become followers of Jesus Christ really doubt that God is real. As a matter of fact, if you have received the Lord Jesus, you know He is real. The problem many people seem to have is accepting where God has them in life. They do not have trouble believing Him; they just cannot believe where He has them. It reminds me of the children of Israel as God was leading them to the Promised Land. God had delivered them with miraculous power from the hands of an obstinate Pharoah. They had witnessed the ten plagues and the death of the first-born of Egypt. They had witnessed the Egyptian army as they were swallowed alive in the Red Sea by the power of God. They saw God turn bitter water into precious drinking water as Moses cast a tree into it at the command of the Lord.

After all of these miracles, the Word of God reveals something very interesting in Exodus 16:

Then the Lord said to Moses, "Behold, I will rain bread from heaven for you; and the people shall go out and gather a day's portion every day, that I may test them, whether or not they will walk in my instruction. And it will come about on the sixth day, when they prepare what they bring in, it will be twice as much as they gather daily." So Moses and Aaron said to all the sons of Israel, "At evening *you will know that the Lord has brought you out* of the land of Egypt." (verses 4–7)

Wait a minute. Do you mean to tell me that they were not convinced God was responsible for the miracles they had witnessed? I do not believe for a moment they were that ignorant. They believed God had brought them out; they just could not believe where He had brought them! So it is with God's children. We do not have as much trouble believing Him as we do believing where He has us. The Israelites did not like where God had brought them. They did not like the twists and turns God had allowed in their lives. Because they were not living by faith, they lived with haunting, daunting questions spawned in hell. Can't you hear their thoughts? We are going to die of thirst! We will never have meat to eat. We were better off in Egypt. If we move ahead, we will drown in the Red Sea. If we stand here, we will die at the hands of the Egyptian army.

Where was their faith? It was in the same place as many Christians. It was buried beneath the desires of hearts yielded to the flesh. Jesus our Lord went to Gethsemane lifting up the shield of faith! He knew the cross would work together for His Father's glory and His good (and ours). The devil probably told Him He deserved better than a cross. I believe He wielded the shield of faith looking toward Sunday morning and a resurrection! By faith, He looked ahead to a church blazing a trail of salvation in His name! Yes, faith does have victory, doesn't it?

Has it ever occurred to you that faith is useless if there is nothing to trust Him for? Usually, there needs to be a need before we need faith. The Bible teaches it is impossible to please God without faith (Hebrews 11:6). If you combine those two thoughts, you will quickly learn that it is during times of immense uncertainty and pain that we have the opportunity and privilege to really please our King. It is during these times that God gives us extraordinary opportunities to please Him.

I am not a trained psychologist or psychotherapist, but I wonder how many Christian people diagnosed with panic attacks and other panic disorders are in need of a little more donning of their spiritual armor? Have we really taken seriously the reality of spiritual warfare? Why are so many people having panic and manic episodes? I might be wrong, but I believe many Christians diagnosed with these disorders need a little time in Bible study. They need some application as well. They need to stop living life spiritually naked. I do not believe this to be true for every case but for many of them.

Are you seeking the Lord and consistently putting on the whole armor of God? We need faith. Too many are going out into the battle partially clad. When the devil sinks the venomous fangs of disbelief into your life, he will inject anxious thoughts that are able to paralyze you with haunting fears. God wants you to apply the antidote of prayer that is able to give mind-boggling peace (Philippians 4:6–7). "The name of the Lord is a strong tower, the righteous run into it and are safe" (Proverbs 18:10). How else does one run into it (Him) but by faith?

How is your faith? The Bible adjures you to take up the shield of faith. Strap it on the forearm by faith, and you will be able to extinguish all of the enemy's flaming arrows. They are fiery because they come from hell. God gives you the choice of strapping on the water-saturated shield of faith or the petroleum-saturated shield of fear and disbelief. How is your faith? The water of faith extinguishes. The fuel of fear ignites. How is your faith?

Scriptures

What soldier is effective in battle without some form of attack or offensive capability? God has not left us unprepared in our struggle. We have the weapon of God's Word, the sword of the Spirit. Second Corinthians 10:3–6 states, "For the weapons of our warfare are not carnal, but divinely powerful for the destruction of fortresses" (New American Standard). Hebrews 4:12 proclaims, "For the Word of God is living and active and sharper than any two-edged sword, and piercing as far as the division of the soul and spirit, and both joints and marrow, and able to judge the thoughts and actions of the heart" (New American Standard). Yes, the Bible is a mighty tool in our struggle for godliness and faithfulness through difficult times. Many might ponder the difference between the truth of God's Word in verse 17 and the truth with which we are to gird our loins from verse 14. Remember, verse 14 refers to a desire to conform one's life to the truth of God's will. It is the determination to live within the parameters of God's Word as a whole. On the other hand, the sword of the Spirit refers to particular verses of the Word of God. There is the life lived within the parameters and boundaries of God's Word, and that life is to be lived according to the specific will of God, revealed through particular verses in the Bible.

Certainly, Jesus lived a life with His loins girded with truth. He defines the meaning of girding one's loins saying, "My meat is to do the will of Him that sent Me, and to finish His work" (John 4:34). Our Lord Jesus' heart was intent upon living within the boundaries of His Father's will. However, when tempted to sin and venture outside those parameters, Jesus wielded the sword of the Spirit to dispel Satan's schemes. Matthew 4 illustrates His mastery of the sword when Jesus answers every demonic call to sin with specific verses relative to the specific temptation. If your

126

loins are not girded with truth, you will not have the heart to detect Satan's wiles. If you do not have a hand on the sword, you will not have the artillery necessary to match the enemy's assault. Having your loins girded about with truth enables you to detect error; the sword helps you to deflect error.

When you go through the fire, you might struggle with feelings of anger or bitterness. Take up the sword of the Spirit in Ephesians 4:31–32 where the Word states, "Let all bitterness and wrath and anger and clamor and slander be put away from you, along with all malice. And be kind to one another, tenderhearted, forgiving each other, just as God in Christ also has forgiven you" (New American Standard). Perhaps you have suffered the loss of a job or dream. The devil works overtime to discourage and lead you to despair. Take up the sword from Jeremiah 29:11 where the Word says, "For I know the plans that I have for you," declares the Lord, "plans for welfare and not for calamity to give you a future and a hope" (New American Standard). Imagine someone close to your heart dies and Satan whispers, "Your best days are behind you now. Life will never be sweet again." Wield the sword of God's Word from Psalm 16:11: "In Thy presence is fullness of joy; at Thy right hand there are pleasures for evermore."

As you might imagine, it takes some time in the Word to get a hand on the handle of the sword. I cannot stress enough the necessity of Scripture memorization and meditation. Saturate your life with the Word of God. The inclination for mature Christians is to become satisfied with the verses they have memorized over the years. What is the last verse you memorized? What verse are you currently working on? You never know when you will need the weapon of God's Word. If you are intent on neglecting your time with God, you will see the devil running roughshod over you. You will see victory only when you get serious about learning and obeying the truth of the Word of God.

Too many believers are going around with empty sheaths. Too often the enemy finds us empty-handed and vulnerable. I wonder how our lives would change if we spent as much time with the Bible as we do surfing the Internet or reading the newspaper. If you can remember the lyrics of songs, then you can memorize the precious Word of God. The real problem is motivation. Are you tired of allowing the devil to capitalize on your anemic walk with God? Get serious about Bible study and Scripture memorization.

Before we leave this chapter, I want you to think about how often you face the day spiritually naked or partially clad for battle. As you would not leave your home naked, do not go out to face another day without your spiritual clothing. The urgency comes from Ephesians 6:11 and 6:13. Without the armor of God, you will not be able to resist or stand firm. The resolve to spend quantity time with the Lord comes from verses 11 and 13 as well. The Bible says, "Put on the full armor of God." It takes time to get dressed, doesn't it? How is your time with the Lord? A Christian partially clad will be spiritually sad. A Christian fully clad will be spiritually glad!

Chapter 11

MOPE, DOPE, ROPE, OR HOPE?

"For I reckon that the sufferings of this present time are not worthy to be compared with the glory which shall be revealed in us." (Romans 8:18)

Right now, some of you are realizing that I skipped part of the armor in the last chapter. I did this purposefully because I want to devote a whole chapter on the subject of hope. Hope is the forgotten element in our Christian pilgrimage. Our blessed hope rests in our heritage where from an old rugged cross blasts the triumphant Word of God saying, "We have won!" Our hope rests upon this unalterable foundation and gives us certainty as the children of God that **the best is yet to come!** Our hope rests in the spiritual heritage; that same hope arrests our hearts and minds when the circumstances of life get beyond our control and seemingly beyond His as well. Ephesians 6:17 commands, "Take the helmet of salvation." The helmet of salvation is a protective device worn on the head to protect our thinking. Has the devil ever played mind-games with you? The helmet is afforded us because we have received salvation. As a result of God's salvation, there is hope!

When trials come, people endure in various ways. The choices are basic: mope, dope, rope, or hope. Some get depressed and begin to mope around. Others turn to dope (or something similar). Some commit suicide. The wise turn to God in hope. Before I knew the Lord, I tried the first two and gave thought to the third a time or two. If you have never settled the question as to where you will spend eternity, I plead with you to trust Jesus Christ. He has never disappointed me or let me down. He provides real hope for the present and future. As a believer, hope provides fertile soil apt to produce acres of lush spiritual growth that honors God and causes those around us to hunger for the God we know. Because of the hope and happiness Jesus provides, life is worth living. I concur with the song, "He's the only reason I live, but, oh, what a reason!"

Life can be relentlessly difficult at times. I thank God there will not be a time in this life that I will have more of His precious presence than I currently have. Jesus is always with me. The Lord's presence in our lives does not fluctuate. Just as God was in the fiery furnace with those three Jewish zealots, I am grateful for His presence in the fiery trials of life. As God provides strength for the journey, He also provides stamina for the journey! He will give you what you need to go, and He will give you what you need to keep going!

You might not be able to relate to this, but sometimes I get weary and tired. Frankly, I get to the point where I have had enough. If you cannot relate to this in some degree, you probably have not been entrusted with significant personal adversity. It might be that you are squeezing an unhealthy amount of satisfaction from this world. As for me, I am hungry to go home now more than ever. Yes, life has its wonderful moments. I agree with C. S. Lewis when he says, "Our Father refreshes us on the journey with some pleasant inns, but will not encourage us to mistake them for home."[1] Having His graceful provisions are real, timely, and sufficient, but I get tired of the affairs of this world. I believe I have a healthy dissatisfaction with our worldly existence.

Christians in America are so inebriated with what this world has to offer that they are not hungry for heaven. Why are we so content with a partial view and understanding of God? When we get to heaven, we will see Him as He is (1 John 3:2). Our church projects our beloved pastor on two big screens as he is preaching on Sundays. One morning as I was watching Pastor Johnny on the big screen, God said, "Why are you so content to look indirectly at him on the screen when you could be looking directly at him?" I turned my eyes to the pulpit. Then God said, "I wish My church was not so content knowing Me indirectly." I thank God for the indirect knowledge, but I'm looking forward to seeing Him face to face (1 Corinthians 13:12). We know Him now through the screen of faith, but one day we will look directly upon Him!

Yes, God is good all the time, but life's circumstances are not. I am thankful He makes me able to respond to life as if it were good all the time. The rest areas of joy along this long and winding journey toward our eternal abode are wonderful indeed. The birth of a baby, the marriage of two souls, the salvation of a friend, the healing of a mother's illness, a child's graduation, the purchase of a new home—all of these are times of immense joy and satisfaction. Despite the joys of life, the intense jolts of life serve to remind us a better day is coming. They remind us that we are to be looking for and longing for another time and another place. Malcolm Muggeridge says, "The only ultimate tragedy in life is to feel at home here."² God will attempt to keep us from forgetting this world is not our home. Life can be difficult, and God has not left us to despair. There is hope!

The Bible teaches us to be "looking for that blessed hope, and the glorious appearing of the great God and Savior Jesus Christ" (Titus 2:13). As a pastor and as an itinerant preacher, I do not know of an area of Christian neglect more prevalent than the neglect of our blessed hope in His return. Have you ever thought about the fact that the word hope is a noun as well as a verb? Hope is something we are to do, and it is something we are to embrace. Hope is something we are to actively do, and it is something we are to affectionately desire! For the follower of Jesus Christ, our hope involves several things. Regarding the topic of adversity, I want to focus on the one aspect of our hope that has the most pertinent implications. Our hope in the return of Jesus Christ to rapture the church is part of the Christian hope. You are to be looking for the dawn of this grand moment! Hope is a future event with present ramifications and implications. The return of Jesus Christ in the air to rapture the church is a future certainty, and we ought to be impacted by it greatly in the here and now!

The rapture is just one part of a series of events that comprise what the Bible terms the second coming of Jesus Christ. The second coming of the Lord Jesus Christ will commence with the rapture of the church. According to 1 Thessalonians 4:13–17, the rapture is the event when Jesus comes in the air to take His saints out of this world before the great tribulation begins. I know there are many God-loving, Bible-believing followers of Jesus Christ who do not embrace the pre-tribulation rapture of the church. But let me engage you for a moment regarding the rapture of the church, because it is intricately related to the value of our hope.

Titus 2:13 regards His return as blessed. Wherein is the blessedness of this doctrine? It is blessed because of the hope it instills in the Christian heart. The rapture of the church is the event that will remove believers from the strife of life. At that moment, our battles will be over! Except for those who will be saved during the great tribulation, it is the event that will end Christian misery in this world of woe. We do not know the time it will occur. In His infinite wisdom, God has left us uninformed as to the date. We have something grand and glorious to wake up with every day—the possible imminent return of Jesus our Lord!

I do not embrace the rapture of the church as a mid or post-tribulation event because it negates the virtue and value of the rapture as *our* blessed hope. A mid or post-tribulation rapture would enable the people God saves during the great tribulation to map their way through it with the aid of God's Word in the Revelation. They would be able to pinpoint the rapture and His return. *This would only be a hope for believers in the great tribulation.* The hope of His return is something Christians of all time can look for with certainty, although there is an unknown element—the date. We look forward to His return in the air before the great tribulation. Those who receive Christ as Lord during the great tribulation will have His return to the earth as their blessed hope! Therefore, we have something real and glorious to embrace. We can awaken every day and live with the glorious possibility that today might be the day the Son of God cracks the eastern sky and rescues us from this world of woe and takes us to that place where sin and Satan will be no more!

The value of our hope in His return exists in the fruit it produces. Knowing my calendar has a week set aside for vacation helps me get through the present. We have an eternal vaca-

tion awaiting us, which will commence with the rapture. God
has set aside the time. There are many ways the Second Coming
should impact our lives. With regard to our trials, hope in His
Second Coming should give us the ability to keep on going
despite the relentless winds of adversity, heartache, and disappointment. Meditate on the Word of God:

> "He giveth power to the faint; and to them that have no
> might He increaseth strength. Even the youths shall faint
> and be weary, and the young men shall utterly fall: But they
> that wait upon the Lord shall renew their strength; they shall
> mount up with wings as eagles; they shall run, and not be
> weary; and they shall walk, and not faint" (Isaiah 40:29–31).

Did you notice the *appropriation* of our hope? To wait on
the Lord is to hope in the Lord. For the Jewish listeners of Isaiah's
day, they were a beleaguered people learning of their impending doom and exile at the hands of the Babylonians. They had
received the prophetic word from God of a promised Messiah.
The prospects of His coming were to be a tremendous source of
strength for the Jews of Isaiah's day. Furthermore, these verses
are to be a great source of strength and stamina for us as well,
for they have their ultimate fulfillment in His Second Coming!

The *anchor* of our hope is Jesus Christ. The Bible says,
"Those who hope for the Lord." Jesus Christ is the Lord, and
we are to hope in Him and His return! Hope is the manner in
which we appropriate this anchor. We live every day with our
hearts cognizant of His possible return. We wait. We hope. We
look. We know our rescue might be at any moment. I have
spent many nights staring intently at the tip of a fishing rod
awaiting the bite of a catfish. I have sat on uncomfortable, rocky
shorelines for hours awaiting a bite. How much more are we to
live with the patient, intense, intent gaze toward the eastern sky

for His glorious appearance? As we sit in the uncomfortable banks of this life, we need to appropriate the cushion of His imminent return!

There are sure *advantages* for those who wait upon the Lord. The Bible teaches we will renew our strength (verse 31). Waiting for His coming will renew your strength to levels you had before trials and difficulties found you. You will be able to "mount up with wings as eagles" (verse 31). The word mount means you will sprout eagle's wings. As an eagle might fly high enough not to hear cars on a highway or the rushing water of a river, you will be enabled to soar above the very sound of your troubles. These wings will enable flight so high that you will be taken above the problems that stalk your peace of mind. It is quiet at high altitudes. You will be able to have a peace of mind soaring above the fray of this world. You might see your troubles from high altitudes but you will not succumb to them. You will enjoy the altitudinal advantage of being high enough to see the big picture. This will help you maintain your perspective. With eagle's wings, you will fly to such emotional and spiritual heights as to live without concern and care. You will be enabled to carry on with renewed vigor and vitality! You will be able to continue and finish the race set before you (Hebrews 12:1–2).

All of us need the advantages of this blessed hope, for the Bible says, "Even the youths shall faint and grow weary" (Isaiah 40:30). Regardless of your emotional make-up, everyone needs this God-given strength and stamina at one time or another. You can "run and be weary" (verse 31). Even world-class athletes run and get tired. But the appropriation of your hope will enable you with stamina beyond mere world-class athleticism— you will be a heaven-class athlete. You will win the gold for God's glory! You will "walk and not become faint" (vs. 31). You will be able to walk as far as God determines without weariness or fatigue! You will not give in, give up, or give out! You will be the type of athlete who will attract a full house to the Madison Square Garden of your life. They will come, and they will watch as God uses your wings to confound the minds of a skeptical world. They will stand in awe of Jesus Christ as you salt them and shine on them (Matthew 5:13–16). Some will see your good works and glorify your Father in heaven!

When I think of the advantages of our hope, I am reminded of Mother Teresa's response to a question regarding her times of suffering as a missionary in India for several decades. She said, "When we get to heaven, all our worst experiences on earth will seem like no more than a bad night in a cheap motel."[3] Isn't that what God led Paul to write in Romans 8:18? "For I reckon that the sufferings of this present time are not worthy to be compared with the glory which shall be revealed in us." The glory will be revealed when our hope is finally realized—at the second coming of our Lord Jesus!

I want you to study the impact and the advantage such thinking had on the apostle Paul. You will not believe his attitude despite his problems. Paul's embracement of this cardinal doctrine had an astounding impact on his perspective toward life. The Holy Spirit led the great missionary to record some of his trials as a Christian in 2 Corinthians 11:23:

> "Are they ministers of Christ? (I speak as a fool) I am more; in labors more abundant, in stripes above measure, in prisons more frequent, in deaths oft. Of the Jews five times received I forty stripes save one. Thrice I was beaten with rods, once I was stoned, thrice I suffered shipwreck, a night and a day I have been in the deep; In journeyings often, in perils of robbers, in perils by mine own countrymen, in perils by heathen, in perils in the city, in perils in the wilderness, in perils in the sea, in perils among false brethren; In weariness and

painfulness, in watchings often, in hunger and thirst, in fastings often, in cold and nakedness. Beside those things that are without, that which cometh upon me daily, the care of all the churches."

Now, I want you to compare Paul's itemized list of troubles with his God-given perspective toward these trials that he gives in 2 Corinthians 4:16–18: "For which cause we faint not; but though our outward man perish, yet the inward man is renewed day by day. For our light affliction which is but for a moment, worketh for us a far more exceeding and eternal weight of glory; while we look not at the things which are seen: for the things which are seen are temporal; but the things which are not seen are eternal."

Before Paul ever disclosed the itemized list of his trials in chapter 11, he gave his perspective toward them in 2 Corinthians 4:17 as *light*. Light affliction? How did he see such great and frequent misfortunes as light? He gives a partial answer in verse 17 as well, "For light affliction which is but for a moment." He saw his trials as merely *temporary*. Our attitudes would change drastically if we would remind ourselves often that a better day is coming—that this life is not all there is. Thank God, a better day is coming! The Bible says, "And God shall wipe away all tears from their eyes; And there shall be no more death, neither sorrow, nor crying, neither shall there be any pain: for the former things are passed away" (Revelation 21:4).

Paul further explains his attitude in Romans 8:18 saying, "For I reckon that the sufferings of this present time are not worthy to be compared with the glory which shall be revealed in us." He saw his problems as momentary. He viewed them as minute in light of his glorious inheritance in heaven! Yes, friend, things will get better—some day. We know the best is always

137

yet to come for the children of God! As a loving parent rushes in to embrace and comfort a child awakened with a bad dream, so, too, will Jesus Christ rush to our aid at His Second Coming! We will be swept into the arms of the Almighty and gently cuddled at His breast for all eternity. The nightmares will be over. Then we will serve Him. Our rest in eternity will be so sweet that any possible thought of our earthly struggles will seem insignificant and unworthy of our attention.

Chapter 12

THE WARSHIP OF WORSHIP

August is a wonderful time to visit the Florida Gulf Coast, especially when the weather is good. A couple of years ago, Lisa and I planned a trip to Panama City Beach. The day before our departure, I put the luggage carrier on top of our van. Later in the day, I was sitting at my computer working on some administrative issues for the ministry while Lisa was out shopping for our vacation. When she arrived home, I heard the garage door rising and there was an awful noise that seemed to shake the house. She forgot the luggage carrier was on top of the van when she pulled into the garage. It was not a pretty sight. Well, that night I heard about a tropical storm that was developing and moving toward the Gulf Coast. By the next morning, the storm was nearing hurricane strength and moving toward Panama City Beach. We decided to trust the Lord with it, right?

We departed for sunny Florida about mid-afternoon. Lisa and I were a little concerned when we began to notice nearly every car going in the opposite direction. We were traveling south; they were traveling north. About the only car going south was the one that pulled up beside us on the interstate with the driver waving and sounding the horn to get our attention. I pulled over in the rain and wind to discover our luggage carrier was opened and almost emptied. Apparently, Lisa's little accident the day before had damaged the lock. We counted our losses and resumed our journey.

The weather deteriorated more and more the closer we got to the coast. When we arrived in Panama City Beach, the winds were gusting to hurricane force. Having never been in a strong tropical storm or a category-one hurricane, Lisa wanted to go with me to the beach. As I put the car in park, I remember her saying, "Look at the wind! Doesn't it make you want to get out in it?" When she opened the door to get out of the van, a perfectly timed gust of wind nearly tore the door off its hinges. I helped her close it, and then I had to use a cord to secure the door. The rain was able to come into the van and soak the carpet the carpet. It began to smell really good throughout the week. We were blessed that the body repair shop only charged us a few hundred dollars to weld the door back on the hinges.

Now, I hope you were blessed by that little story because it vividly reminds me of a time when God was testing the quality of my worship. It was an inconvenient experience, and I am sure the devil was pleased with the way I reacted (not responded). We have an enemy who is bent on ruining and wrecking our lives. Satan wants to taint and tarnish our testimonies. He has a plan and many backup plans to discourage, dissuade, and destroy you. Listen to Jesus again when He says, "The thief comes *only* to steal, kill, and destroy" (John 10:10). The thief is Satan, and He has only one agenda. He wants to engage us on this sea called the Christian life, and He will not rest until we are sunk. Worship is the warship by which Christ's followers are enabled to disable and destroy the battleship of Satan's plan. He seeks to sink blood-bought vessels called believers who have set sail on the sea of life for the glory of Jesus Christ!

I am convinced that the church in America is largely in the dark about the meaning of worship. *Worship is giving all that we are to all that He is all the time.* Worship is not merely some thing we gather to do on Sundays. It is not merely singing the songs of God or praises to Him. Worship is something we come together to do having been doing it all week in order to depart and continue doing it! We come together doing it individually, to do it corporately, in order to go out doing it individually.

Worship is the warship by which we sink the plans of the devil to thwart God's glory in the world. Walt Disney made a movie titled, "20,000 Leagues Beneath the Sea". The movie involved a ship that was built with sharp and pointed blades on the exterior. The jagged exterior was designed to the cut through enemy vessels as the captain raced the ship at high rates of speed. Every time the captain found the enemy, he would increase the speed of the ship and plow ahead cutting the enemy ship asunder and sending them to the bottom of the sea. Make a special note of this point—between you and the devil—someone is going to sink. Jesus dealt Satan a fatal and final blow at Calvary, but his ship is still going under. Even though he is fatally wounded, the devil is still fighting. The great ship Titanic did not sink for over a hour after striking an iceberg. The ship did not tilt immediately upon running into it. Even the lights inside the ocean-liner remained on until not long before she sank to the bottom of the sea. Satan is the same way. He might seem alive and well, but He is on his way down. He is mortally wounded. He has lost. He is a defeated foe.

If you want to plow through Satan and his schemes, regardless of what you go through in life, worship is the only alternative. Worship is much more involved than most of us realize. I want to spend a good deal of time on the subject because the battle is won and lost here. I do not know of a better portion of Scripture regarding the subject than Romans 12:1–2. Read these verses carefully: "I urge you, therefore, brethren, by the mercies of God, to present your bodies a living and holy sacrifice, acceptable to God, which is your spiritual service of worship. And do not be conformed to this world, but be transformed by the renewing of your mind, that you may prove what the will of God is, that which is good, acceptable and perfect" (New American Standard).

The Exhortation for Our Worship

The context of Romans 12:1–2 is worship. God exhorts us to live lives of worship. The Bible says in verse one, "I *urge* you." These words are written as if God is grabbing us by the spiritual neck and attempting to shake us and wake us. Why does God urge us and beseech us to worship? Worship is intricately and intrinsically linked with the will of God. Our ability to discern His will is directly aligned with holiness and obedience. Worship is holiness and obedience. These verses include a three-fold description of God's will as good, acceptable, and perfect.

God exhorts us so strongly because He knows His plan for our lives. He knows every large and minute detail; it is a wonderful plan. He so urges us to worship Him because if we knew His will for our lives the way He knows His will, we would feel foolish doing anything else but giving all that we are to all that He is all of the time! It is only those who worship Jesus Christ who enter His perfect will *and* have the certainty of it.

As we shall learn, worship is the path that leads directly to the path of God's perfect will. The Bible says, "Thy Word is a lamp unto my feet and a light unto my path" (Psalm 119:105). As we live our lives in accordance to the Word of God, God will show us the decisions to make in the here and now (feet) and down the road (path). He will show you what to do now and later, near and down the road! You will be in His will, and it is never disappointing!

The problem is that too many of God's children are content with experiencing less than the Master has planned for them. Some are content with a good life when God has a good and acceptable plan for them. Some are content with a good and acceptable life when God has a good, acceptable, and perfect will for them. Too often we are content eating crumbs from the floor of God's permissive will when He would have us to feast on the filet mignon of His perfect will. Someone stated it well, saying, "The enemy of best is good." Usually, what separates us from His perfect will is one thing—worship. If only you could see what God has in store for you, you would rush toward a lifestyle of worshipping Jesus Christ! You would understand the urgency of God's Word.

The Encouragement for Our Worship

God gives the great motivating factor for our worship in verse one when He says, "By the mercies of God." The mercy of God is a great source of motivation and encouragement for us to really give all that we are to all that He is every day of our lives. Inherent in the idea of mercy is that God will never treat us as our sins deserve. If you have received Jesus Christ as your personal Lord and Savior, you will never experience the consequences of your sin because of God's mercy. In His mercy, Jesus went to Calvary and died on the cross in order to experience the wrath of God toward our sins. Now, we may celebrate with Psalm 103:10, which states, "He has not dealt with us according to our sins, nor rewarded us according to our iniquities." If He were not such a compassionate God, Jesus would have left us to pay for our sinful indebtedness. Thanks be unto God for His merciful alternative, "He saved us, not on the basis of deeds which we have done in righteousness, but according to His mercy, by the washing of regeneration and renewing of the Holy Spirit" (Titus 3:5).

The mercy of God teaches me that I can pay for my sins or trust that Jesus Christ paid for them at Calvary nearly 2000 years ago. The reason I will never experience what my sins deserve is because Jesus experienced they deserve! God will never treat me as my sins deserve. He did not treat me as my sins deserved before I was saved, and He will not do it now that I am saved. Jesus experienced what I deserved on my behalf. That is the mercy of God. Romans 12:1 teaches it ought to be a major source of encouragement to worship Jesus Christ. Think about it—Jesus gave all He was for us. It is not unreasonable that we should give all we are to Him! Take time to ponder the mercies of God. If it does not motivate you and encourage you to worship Him with all that you are, then you have a good reason to question whether you have genuinely experienced His mercy.

The Expectation of Our Worship

In Romans 12:1–2, God reveals His will for our lives as the children of God. He expects us to worship Him. Verse one proceeds saying, "That you present." God expects every one of us to present ourselves to Him for worship. I have met some people who claim to be in a personal, saving relationship with Jesus Christ, and they continue to live for themselves. Have you met anyone who thinks the day they were saved was the end? The moment God saved us was only the beginning. It was not the end, but rather the beginning of something. God expects us to present ourselves to Him for His use every moment of our lives. If you are a child of God, Jesus now expects you to present yourself to Him. Our presentation to Him in worship is to be a consistent lifestyle. It is not to be determined and dictated by the issues we are facing or the trials we are encountering. The Christian life is not about having a quiet time with God in the morning and rushing off to meet the challenges of the day on our own. The day is His, and worship is to extend throughout every minute of the day. God expects you to present yourself to Him in order to give all that you are to all that He is every moment of every day! That is worship, and it is His expectation.

The Extent of Our Worship

The reason I define worship as giving all that we are is found in the verse one where the Bible uses the word *bodies*. Does God expect us to present merely our physical faculties to Him? No, the Word of God employs this language as a means of conveying the extent to which we are to worship Jesus Christ. The word encompasses and envelops all that we are in every realm. Our worship is to know no boundaries, and is to extend to every area of our lives—physical, emotional, spiritual, material, mental, academic, social, and vocational. Name any realm of your existence, and God expects your worship of Him to extend into that area. You are to give all that you are to all that He is all of the time. Even when life is really difficult in one area, and God has allowed some terrible tragedy to touch that realm, still, He expects your worship.

God has a good way of revealing the extent of our worship. Just let Him dry up our finances, allow a bad grade, or send a physical ailment, and you will see the ways you have never really given those areas of your life to Him in worship. Bitterness and resentment reveal the heart of one who has reserved a few things for their personal consumption (and worship). But true worship gives God every area of one's existence and being. Worship says, "Lord, take all of me and all pertaining to me, and do with me as You please. Bankrupt me, take my health, or let me lose my job. I will bring You honor in and through these hardships. I give all that I am to all that You are no matter what." That is extensive worship, and that is what God expects.

There was a hen and pig walking down the street of a small town in the mid-west. They stopped in front of the town café and began reading a sign promoting a breakfast special. The sign read, "Ham/Egg Special $2.99." The pig asked the hen, "What do you think about that?" The hen replied, "It doesn't bother me very much." The pig quickly said, "I guess not. For you, it's just a donation. For me, it's a full commitment."

There is one pivotal question for every saved person to answer, "Am I making donations to the Lord with areas of my life, or am I making a full commitment?" Are you totally surrendered and yielded to the Lord? Are you totally submitted? It is the only extent of worship that is acceptable to God.

The Essence of Our Worship

How would you describe your Christian life? What is the essence of it? How would those who best know you describe your life? What characterizes your Christian life? What is the essence of it? Your answer will go a long way in determining whether you are a worshipper. Romans 12:1 defines the essence of our worship as "a living sacrifice." Sacrificial living is what characterizes one leading a life of worship. Sacrifice for the Christian is positive teaching with a negative connotation. I like hearing my wife tell me that I am the best husband a woman could possibly desire. I melt when I hear my sons telling me I'm the best daddy they have ever had—well, I think I know what they mean. However, I live that they might see me as a sacrifice unto the Lord Jesus Christ. By the way, if you get the horse of sacrifice pulling the cart of your life, you will be all you could hope to be in this life.

Living sacrificially is a positive lifestyle, because it is only in the dying that we ever truly experience life in the first place. There is one negative connotation—it will require something of us that we might not otherwise desire to depart and relinquish. If there is not some struggle reminiscent of a modern day Gethsemane where you chose His way rather than your own, then you are probably cheating yourself out of true Christian worship.

Think of the last time you went through a difficult series of events. If you chose to love God and honor Him through the trial, deferring your rights and your preferences for His mysterious way, then you were probably worshipping Jesus Christ. Sacrifice often entails dying to our preferences and the way we would like to see things go. Just as our Lord Jesus lay across the rock at Gethsemane, we should lay our hearts upon the anvil of sacrifice, choosing His way and will over our own. The primary issue can never be whether we deserve this treatment or that. Of utmost importance is our worship of Jesus Christ through it: how can I be a sacrifice in this circumstance? It is to be the essence of your walk with Him.

The Evidence of Our Worship

The sure sign that you are worshipping Jesus Christ is the change He is bringing to your heart, life, and character. The characteristics of your life will be revolutionized. Your demeanor will change, and your response to life's pressures will change. Holiness will replace ungodliness. Unwholesome habits will be replaced with wholesome habits. Regardless of your circumstances, you will have a good perspective and response as you worship Jesus. The evidence of worship is change. Romans 12:2 states, "But be transformed by the renewing of your mind." It is worship that transforms us. We begin to see and acknowledge the ways we have conformed to this world. Worship translates into the surrender by which the Holy Spirit controls us and produces the transforming fruit of the Spirit. It is change from the inside out.

My wife challenged me a couple of years ago. Our family was going through a time of systematic aggravations and inconveniences. One day I responded in a certain manner and she said, "You've been saved too long to still be talking like that." Well, if you had asked my opinion about my walk with God, I would have been pretty proud of it. But Lisa was right. Change is the evidence of a life of worship. My lips revealed the lack of depth in my worship. Adversity has a way of providing us opportunity to see where we are spiritually at a given moment. Sometimes we miss the point God is trying to make unless we have someone there to sharpen our iron (Proverbs 27:17). You can believe all you want about the health of your fellowship with Jesus, but the sure sign of that health is change. Worship is recognizable by a transformed heart that leads to a changed life. It is the evidence.

The Enabling of Our Worship

One of the great personal benefits of our worship is what it enables us to do. Worship enables one to *sort* out the will of God. Romans 12:2 says, "But be transformed by the renewing of your mind, that you may *prove* what the will of God is." God's Word teaches that we are enabled to prove His will when we are worshipping Jesus Christ. To prove His will is to sort through the numerous opportunities often placed before us. Sometimes we are left with several doors of opportunity. There are times that you will go through a difficult time and there will be several roads of response from which to choose. How does one make the correct choice with confidence, regardless of the gravity of the situation surrounding the decision? Worship is the key.

Let's face it—some trials are the result of making the wrong choices. Once we have made a wrong choice, where do we turn to rectify the circumstance? How do we get out? It is like Scarlett O'Hara's famous question for Rhett Butler in *Gone With the Wind*, "But Rhett, where will I go, and what shall I do?" Be thankful God never answers in the same infamous manner Rhett did!

Other circumstances are not the result of sin. They are the trials God sends to prune, promote, or portray us. These situations require decisions as well. They are not the result of a bad decision, but a bad decision could lead to our lingering there a little longer than we would care to. How does one know what direction to take? Sometimes it is very difficult to discern.

You always have one choice to make—worship. As you give all that you are to all that He is each and every moment, God will give you the innate spiritual sense to know the path to follow. The Bible teaches, "The steps of a good man are ordered of the Lord" (Psalm 37:23). When you are worshipping Jesus, yielded and surrendered, the Holy Spirit will show you the way you should go. His Word will be a lamp to your *feet*, showing you the immediate steps to take (Psalm 119:105). His Word will be a light to your *path* enabling you to be prepared for what is down the road. Worship enables us to make the right decisions, and sometimes it is the decision to make no decision—to keep doing what you have been doing. Regardless of the circumstances, worship is paramount to flourishing through the trials of life. When you are in it for nothing, you will have a heart of worship and a mind with clear perception. You will hear the sure voice of your Shepherd guiding every move.

The Enjoyment of Our Worship

The most common lie spoken on a regular basis is, "I'm fine." I have told the proverbial lie so many other Christians utter, particularly on Sunday mornings as the church meets. "How are you doing, Scott?" And despite the travail and consternation in my life, I say, "Oh, I'm fine. How are you?" Now, there are times when we do not need to share some issues. But there are moments when we simply are not doing well and the walls seem to be falling in around us. I am sure you would like to be able to look everyone in the eyes and respond to that same question with these words, "Life is great!" Do you realize worship will lead to a life that is great? It is a life of enjoyment.

Romans 12:2 describes God's will as good, acceptable, and perfect. That sounds like a life one could really enjoy. As you worship Jesus Christ, He will lead you into His perfect will that His Word calls good, acceptable, and perfect. *Good* means you will like it. *Acceptable* means you will not want to change it. *Perfect* means you cannot improve it. Would you like to answer honestly the question, "How are doing?" with these words, "It could not get any better." I can honestly write and say, "If life gets any better, I do not know what I will do." I like it, I do not want to change it, and it is perfect! It is the result of being in God's will, that being the result of worship.

No matter which way the road of life turns, down the rocky path of adversity or down the paved road along the mountain stream, God wants me to honor Him. He deserves to be magnified and praised by my life and lips. I must be in it for nothing. Are you in it for nothing? Are you worshipping Jesus, giving all that you are to all that He is all the time? Remember, it is not giving all that you are to all He might give you. Sink Satan's plans with the warship of worship.

When you find yourself in the University of Adversity, keep close watch over your perception of the circumstances. Remember you are not your own but a trophy of His grace! You are His. Respond as did Job when his job was to prove the devil a liar. Live in light of the little boats and prisoners in your life. Be convictable of LUI: Living Under the Influence. Submit, yield, and surrender to the Holy Spirit's control. Abide in Jesus, depending on the same grace that saved you to produce the life of Christ through you. Live in the land of No Can Do. And beware of the enemy. He will attempt to uproot you from abiding there. Live every moment of your life fully clad in the armor God supplies. Rise every day looking for Jesus to split the eastern sky. Have hope in the Lord. The best is yet to come! Give all you are to all He is all the time. Sink the devil. Worship Jesus Christ, and enjoy the outcome—a life that is good, acceptable, and perfect.

Be in it for nothing.

NOTES

Chapter 1
[1] Erwin Lutzer, *The Serpent of Paradise* (Chicago: Moody Press, 1996), 99.
[2] C. S. Lewis, *The Problem of Pain* (HarperCollins Edition, 2001), 31.
[3] Ibid., 48.

Chapter 2
[1] Max Anders, *Spiritual Warfare* (Nashville: Thomas Nelson Publishers, 1997), 9.

Chapter 3
[1] K. P. Yohannan, *The Road to Reality* (Lake Mary, Florida: Charisma House, 1988), 167.
[2] F. B. Meyer, *Tried by Fire* (Christian Literature Crusade, revised edition 1993), 56–57.

Chapter 5
[1] Lutzer, p. 80.
[2] Arthur Pink, *The Attributes of God* (Grand Rapids: Baker Book House, 1975), 9–10.
[3] C. S. Lewis, *The Problem of Pain* (HarperCollins Edition, 2001), 46.

[4] J. Dwight Pentecost, *Your Adversary, the Devil* (Grand Rapids: Zondervan Publishing House, 1969), 88.

Chapter 9
[1] Warren Wiersbe, *The Bible Exposition Commentary*, Volume 2 (Wheaton: Victor Books, 1989), 56.
[2] Judson Cornwall, *Let Us Abide* (Gainesville, Florida: Bridge-Logos Publishers, 1977), 92.

Chapter 11
[1] C. S. Lewis, *The Problem of Pain* (HarperCollins Edition, 2001), 116.
[2] Joseph Stowell, *Shepherding the Church* (Chicago: Moody, 1994), 289.
[3] Max Anders, *Spiritual Warfare* (Nashville: Thomas Nelson, 1997), 90.

For more information regarding DSB Evangelistic Ministries, please consult our website at *http://www.scottbeasley.org/*. We may also be contacted through First Baptist Church Woodstock, Georgia, by calling 770-926-4428.

Suggested Reading

The Holy Bible
Descending Into Greatness by Bill Hybels
A Tale of Three Kings by Gene Edwards
Let Us Abide by Judson Cornwall
The Serpent of Paradise by Erwin Lutzer
The Road to Reality by K. P. Yohannan
How to Worship Jesus Christ by Joseph Carroll
Ablaze for God by Wesley Duewel

ARE YOU SURE THAT YOU ARE GOING TO HEAVEN WHEN YOU DIE?

If you are not certain that you have eternal life and will go to Heaven when you die, there is good news for you! You need to understand three things:

1) <u>You are a sinner, and sin separates you from God</u>. The Bible says in Romans 3:23, "For all have sinned and fallen short of the glory of God." Sin is anything you do that God says not to do. It is anything God says to do that you have not done. Romans 6:23 says, "For the wages of sin is death, but the gift of God is eternal life through Jesus Christ our Lord." Receiving eternal life is like receiving a gift!

2) <u>Jesus is the sinless Son of God, and He died on the cross as payment for your sins</u>. The Bible says in 1 Peter 2:24, "And He bore our sins in His body on the cross." 2 Corinthians 5:21 says, "He (God) made Him who knew no sin to be sin on our behalf, that we might become the righteousness of God in Him." Jesus paid for your sins when He shed His blood and gave His life on the cross nearly 2000 years ago!

3) <u>You must personally accept Jesus' death for your sins by turn</u><u>ing from your sins (repentance) and placing your faith in Christ alone for eternal life</u>. The Bible says in Acts 16:31, "Believe on the Lord Jesus Christ, and you will be saved." John 3:16 says, "For God so loved the world that He gave His only begotten Son, that whoever believes in Him should not perish but have everlasting life."

If you would like to receive the gift of eternal life and accept Jesus Christ as your personal Lord and Savior, pray the following words to God:

> "Lord Jesus, thank you for loving me and dying for me in my place. I should pay for my sins, but You did that for me. I am a sinner. I accept Your death as payment for my sins. I confess You as my Lord, my boss, and I want You to live Your life through me. Cleanse me of all my sins and unrighteousness. I accept You as my righteousness. I believe You are raised from the dead and are alive right now! I die to myself right now. Come into my heart through the person of Your Holy Spirit. Thank you for saving me. Now, teach me to depend upon Your grace and Spirit that You might live Your life through me. In Jesus name I ask. Amen.

If you just prayed to accept Jesus into your heart, please let us know by email (scottbeasl@cs.com) or by phoning: 770-926-4428.

To order additional copies of

in it for N**OTHING**

Have your credit card ready and call:

1-877-421-READ (7323)

or please visit our web site at
www.pleasantword.com

Also available at: www.amazon.com

Printed in the United States
1307100001B/88-342